JADED

To Dream the Impossible Dream

JOHN FERRIS

authorHOUSE®

AuthorHouse™ UK
1663 Liberty Drive
Bloomington, IN 47403 USA
www.authorhouse.co.uk
Phone: 0800.197.4150

Published by AuthorHouse 02/20/2018

ISBN: 978-1-5462-8862-6 (sc)
ISBN: 978-1-5462-8863-3 (e)

CONTENTS

DEDICATION

I dedicate this book to my beautiful wife Karen who has been a pillar of strength throughout our journey and who always gives me enough rope!

I would also like to give a mention to everyone who has been a part of my story especially Jordan and Robyn.

INTRODUCTION

Life... you live, you die, it's inevitable, but for what? From the moment you're born, you're already on your way out. *Perish the thought.* You can dwell on the inevitable and worry about what is just around the corner or you can dream! Me... I'm a dreamer.

Even dreamers can get bored, frustrated and really down on life. At the time of writing I have felt bored and frustrated for quite some time - in a bit of a rut. I am well aware it's up to me and nobody else to drag myself out of the rut. It's all part of the ebb and flow of life. I have come a long way since my life was turned upside down. Tragedy has struck most of us at one time or another. We all deal with it a little differently. To dampen my pain I chose the path of self discovery. It's a strange path to go down – it's like walking along a Möbius strip always returning to the same starting point, never really going anywhere. You go down the rabbit hole and literally end up in Wonderland to discover it's you who is Alice; that all the weirdness is more real than the daily grind you are accustomed to. You discover life is not what you have believed it to be; in fact it's quite the opposite. It's the discovery of how opposites compliment each other which is fundamental to how the *system of life* functions.

I guess what I'm trying to say is, finding out the truth to who we really are and what reality really is can be shocking to most. Responsibility weighs heavy. Not for me. I was in the gutter anyway so I was thrilled by the revelations. I was excited to find out; power comes from within and when activated in the right way can bring about miraculous changes to your life. In saying that, nothing changes that much unless you are prepared to take action. Taking action requires work, not only by introducing a new way of thinking, but also in deleting the sub-conscious programmes that run your old paradigm.

The rut I currently find myself in has nothing to do with my family life. It is more a fatigue in not having attained my ultimate goal, compounded by the frustration of feeling somewhat isolated; adrift from consensual views due to a deeper understanding that few can relate to. For me it's apocalyptic! Sounds over dramatic, but what if I was to inform you the word apocalypse does not mean 'the destruction of the world!' Or at least it didn't originally. People love drama and there's no bigger fear than the old chestnut, the end of the world is nigh!

The book of revelations tells us "The bells ringing ushers in the apocalypse". What this is really saying is "The bells ringing ushers in the revelation of secret knowledge". Therefore the true meaning of the word apocalypse is revelation. How do I know this? Simple sleuthery reveals that the English biblical translations evolved from Coptic Greek. It doesn't matter a jot what the modern interpretation is! It only matters what the Coptic Greek version intended. This is just a simple example of how the world 'out there' manages to pull the veil over your eyes, but it also leads to much bigger questions.

Who and for what reason would deliberately mislead the masses? Simply follow the money trail or follow the power trip. One leads to the money lenders and the other leads to the religious leaders. The Vatican for one has a lot to answer for... imagine! Money and power go hand in hand. They are two sides of the same coin. We all know how money works, but power is more subtle. Power can come in the form of words. By the power of words you have the ability to convince anyone of anything, but with one caveat – they must choose to believe you. Life is a two way street. It's the power of words which keeps you imprisoned, either someone else's or your very own and nothing else. It is all related to the story you tell yourself taking place in your own psyche. Now do you understand why religions twist the meaning of words and phrases to suit their own agendas and why the law society developed a bullshit language that only they fully understand (whilst being lucratively financially rewarded) known as legalese?

There are two threads that run throughout this book. The main thread is an introspective journey of my personal apocalypse and search for my daughter leading to the secret, to not only mine, but your self empowerment too. The second is a more light hearted superficial coming of age story which runs parallel to all the deep shit.

My frustration with life stems from the loss I suffered almost nine years ago and the unfulfilled promise I made. I take full responsibility for my life and blame no one or any circumstance or event for my current situation. Thankfully I'm not the suicidal type, but I can fully appreciate why some beautiful but lost souls take their own lives. The Buddha stated as the first of his four noble truths; that all of life is suffering, pain and misery.

At times he could be a miserable old git! Christians would say thank heavens for Jesus! A man with a brighter outlook on life. I am the light of the world and all that. Me ... I get him, not that I am a Christian. Neither was he for that matter. Life's rollercoaster took me to the metaphorical gates of Hell, my own construction. I've since discovered the devils in you – no prick with horns actually exists! In fact nothing exists except what *you* decide. Herein lies the paradox. If we use God as an example, if you believe a religious God exists you are right, if you don't believe in a religious God you are also right, it's you who decides. Here's the crux – I can say for sure that you believe in some perceived higher power whether you are prepared to admit to it or not. This is our natural essence - you are nowhere and now here somehow at the same time.

I have come to realise and understand that there is a pattern to how life works. I discuss in much greater detail in my book; The Yo(u)niverse Paradox. But knowing isn't doing and doing can be so restricted, not only by others, but by you (in my case forty years of subconscious programming). A battle ensues within me between the older version and the more enlightened one.

"Enlightenment is a destructive process. It has nothing to do with becoming better or being happier. Enlightenment is the crumbling away of untruth. It's seeing through the facade of pretence. It's the complete eradication of everything we imagined to be true"

Adyashanti

Walking the spiritual path is not about being a goody two shoes. It's more like treading a spiralling balance beam which is constantly moving, forever trying to throw you off. On one side you have *this* and on the other *that*. For *this* and *that* to co-exist, you require the 'space in-between', which, when you think about it, is everywhere. *This* and *that* can be objectified as perturbations (deviations of a system) of space, with space in essence being everything and nothing at the same time (dependant on perspective). To blow your mind even more, paradoxically *this* is *that* and *that* is *this* all connected by this spiritual path of spacial nothingness. This is known as a continuum, which is how everything is connected and everything is *one*. If you find this heavy going bear with it. It just might change your life.

The spiritual path is not about bathing in the light and ignoring the darkness. The spiritual path is the *awareness* that without darkness there is no medium for light to exist. Life requires both, it is and will always be dual natured. It takes *time* though, to act on what you know. I've long believed my life lesson is developing patience, upon reading you might discover yours.

"Learn how to see. Realise that everything connects to everything else."

Leonardo Da Vinci

Everything in life *is* connected. This is a long held spiritual view that has been confirmed scientifically through numerous quantum experiments. This unseen quantum wonderland is key to our understanding. Numerous spiritual masters (Jesus, the Buddha, Krishna etc) throughout the ages have told us the answers lie within. (Note: none of the aforementioned spiritual masters where connected to any religion).

"God has no religion."

Mahatma Gandhi

Empathy is our *inner* connection *outwardly* to each other through love. It is love or the lack of that connects all things. Love is the *only* emotion (energy in motion) there truly is, with its opposite being fear. Fear ultimately is the absence of love or where in the moment the least amount of love is experienced. Experience is all you ever do. Life *is* experience, with every outer experience taking place within. Life, love, experience, spirit, God, consciousness or universe... call it what you may, it's all the same. Everything is connected to everything else, whilst at the same time, all being the same. It is all about the perspective taken. You can see it from your ego point of view or you can view it through the god within. At source we really are 'one' big family with each of us being a reflection of each other.

"All things material and spiritual originate from one source and are related as if they were one family"

Morihei Ueshiba

The story that follows is not just my story; It's your story too. How come? From the moment we awaken each day, until we go to sleep at night as well as in our dreams we are all constructing our own personal narratives about who we think we are and who we want to become. A little voice chitters away in the background, that only we ourselves can hear, silenced only on rare occasions when we react to situations, quieten the mind or are in the zone. You could think of this little voice as the story teller. At times you are in control of it, but at others it appears to take control of you. If you want to live the life of your dreams, to dream what others believe to be impossible, then now is the time to take back control; now is the time to let go of your ego; now is the time to become the master of your mind.

COFFEE MAKES YOU POO

It's just another day, in this case, a Saturday. I have been to the gym for a short sharp workout and now have planted myself on a stool by the window of a local coffee shop. As the years have rolled by, I find myself spending a lot more of my time immersed in the coffee shop culture. This phenomenon really took of locally in the mid nineties. It was partially fuelled by the popularity of the F.R.I.E.N.D.S television series, but with Northern Ireland, the whole of Ireland for that matter, known world wide for its pub culture and the prerequisite for social interaction being a pint of the black stuff, I figured it will never last. Little did I know. To be fair it was around the time of the birth of my son Jordan and even though I was well in my twenties I was still a little wet behind the ears. When you're coming out of your teens you think you know everything; when you're coming out of your twenties you have realised you know little. The vastness of the world, its complexities have hit home. For some, the *seeds are being sown* to life's biggest question... who am I? Where did I come from? And for what? I guess this could stem from the birth of the seed that *you* had not long sown!

The trouble and strife has wandered off to the nearby salon to get artificially fried for ten minutes– the vanity of life – me? ... never! Okay well maybe now and again. The coffee shop I find myself in has reopened under new owners. It feels fresh and inviting. I wasn't fussed on the previous one, but this appears to have much better *energy. Time* will tell... *it's a terrible gossip.* The coffee shop is located in Bangor, a small town by the sea, built on a hill near where we live. The two main shopping streets run down and converge at the marina. It's a bit like San Francisco!

Crème Bakehouse

THE PROMISE

My mind wanders. I think about Robyn. It's been almost nine years. I miss her so much. I made Robyn a promise that we would always be together. In those moments you just know in your heart that life is so much more than what is generally accepted. I keep my promises.

My search began 24 hours after the most painful experience I could have imagined. Into the home computer I typed the words 'Parallel Universes'. Why? I guess somewhere deep in my heart where it is connected umbilically to my soul I felt a nudge; to never give up hope no matter the circumstances. The initial search proved fruitless, but in the dying embers a spark ignited, slowly illuminating over the coming years with each new revelation, on my quest to find Robyn.

My Little Princess

Since then I have discovered what I believe is the pattern of life, the pattern to reality itself. Sounds very grandiose, but I am in no doubt. Many *will* doubt though, wondering what makes me so special to be privy to such paramount knowledge. All I can say is I am not special and yet at the same time I am. We are all equal, imbued with the same power and yet at the same time we are all unique and amazing. But to the doubters all I can say is, have you taken the time to ask the deeper questions about life? Do you have the strength of desire to devote years of your life searching, researching, meditating and constantly asking question after question; waiting patiently for the information to enlighten a pattern that includes everything, omitting nothing? I have found the simple pattern that holds all the answers. I'm not having a go at those who don't. We are all at different stages; at different rungs of life's ladder and basically we exist on a '*when we need to know*' basis.

Whether driven by curiosity or tragedy it all starts with the first question. I realised early on if there was any chance of changing the past, to be with my daughter, I inherently knew I had to discover how reality *fundamentally* works. I knew there was no point in looking 'out there' at all the complexities of life, it was all about how things originate and evolve. I cannot stress how important this is. Science makes the critical mistake that if something is decidable, reproducible and falsifiable then this must be what it is and how it is. So what's the mistake in that? Well, the mistake is made when looking outside of yourself at the world at large to discover the answers. What few people know is that science, by its own admission, cannot prove anything is 100% in reality. You see, when you observe 'whatever' and repeat the observation over and over again, what you end up with is a statistical probability of a likely outcome – not a 100% definite one. So why is this? Because what *you* perceive in the world is the outcome of the idea *you* have about it – with no two people having the exact same idea.

The fact the world at large is based on statistical probabilities brings into question its grounding. How can there be a concrete reality if nothing is 100% certain? Heisenberg discovered this in quantum terms, hence his uncertainty principle. This realisation adds credence to the understanding that the answers lie within you and when you ask the deep inner soul-searching questions, the connections begin to appear. The key is understanding that everything is connected at varying scales and when you grasp this, you then have the ability to join the dots to see the fundamental pattern. The key to understanding what life is all about is not just collecting and processing information; when you unlock the mystery of life itself you see the simple fundamental pattern that expresses everything at all scales. This simple pattern allows for every eventuality to unfold. 'Seek and ye shall find' is a spiritual law, not religious doctrine, built into the system. When you awaken to this, there is no going back. How you see the world will have changed forever. Not that you would want to. The victim complex you once clung too evaporates and the ball and chain you have dragged throughout your life slowly crumbles to allow you more freedom to tell a grander story than you ever thought possible.

> *"The two most important days in your life are the day you are born and the day you find out why"*
>
> Mark Twain

To the outside world you appear odd. You do not see the world the way the masses do. When you express your opinions there are some, possibly many, who find it very disconcerting. We all live in a bubble of our own construction and if something or someone comes along and attempts to burst that bubble we feel threatened and exposed. The majority of people are not really interested in the truth. They just want a constant reassurance that what *they* believe is the truth. In my case, a number of friendships have been lost and there's no doubt that others have been distanced. I take full responsibility. It was my choice. I know at times I could become a little overpowering. Karen would say that's enough John and give me the look. I came across the following quote that struck a chord.

> *"A friend is someone who listens to your bullshit, tells you it's bullshit and then listens to more of your bullshit!"*

As time has rolled by, I have become a little wiser in choosing when to speak and when to shut up, but to be honest my intentions were always honourable. I just wanted to help. "A wise man once said nothing" crosses my mind regularly these days, but old habits die hard. Over the years I have learned to tread more carefully. A by-product of this awareness that I had tapped into, was to become, not just more self aware, but also more attuned to the energy of my surroundings and the company I was in.

"Everyone appreciates your honesty, until you're honest with them, then you're an asshole"

George Carlin

THE COLOUR PURPLE

As I sat by the window of the coffee shop admiring the grey drizzle that emanated from our regular cloud covered skies – you do get used to it – I encountered the young waitress for the first time. "Whoa!" was my first thought, not because she is attractive, but by her stunning purple hair. With the dull backdrop coupled with my current grey demeanour, this contrast in colour would be the second time I had experienced an impact of this nature. I'd seen girls with purple hair before and never thought much, but this time it was different. Her hair was cut short at the back with it styled slightly longer on top. I would go so far as to say I have never seen anyone who suited that colour and style as much.

In my youth, I loved girls with blonde hair and dark eyebrows. Back in the day when life was more 'natural' (if you sported a tattoo you were either part of the armed forces or someone who had a propensity for tossing petrol bombs during the troubles... as well as themselves) Karen would usually point out that their hair was obviously dyed. I was usually oblivious to this, but did I care? No. Later, I would have a penchant for longer, darker hair... ok, I'm playing my get out of jail free card here, as you've probably guessed, my wife

Karen is a brunette with hair on the longer side. To be honest though I'm no Brad Pitt so I can't really afford to be *that* fussy.

The young girl standing before me was a futuristic vision of the type of hair colour and style I imagined as a kid would be the norm in today's age. I was brought up on 1970s sci-fi shows such as Space 1999 and U.F.O. The latter had most of the girls wearing *striking* purple wigs. From memory the star of the show was called *Striker...* lucky bastard! Actually, I've just googled it to discover the lead actor played by Ed Bishop was actually called Straker. Well there you go, how your memory plays tricks!

We have all encountered moments when we are totally convinced something happened in a particular way at a certain time or date only to discover that apparently this wasn't the case. Is the past we construct from memory real or could it be we construct our past from our future actions? To most the latter would sound outrageous. In this case the effect would have to happen prior to the cause. It's actually not that outlandish. In today's quantum age retro-causality, to give it its modern title, is now gaining traction from a number of quantum experiments and could be the resolution to many of today's paradoxes.

"Would you like to see a menu or?", "no just two coffee's please". It is quite incredible how much information you process in a fraction of a second. "I love your hair" I blurted out. She looked and flashed the most incredible smile "thank you" she said.

THE ANSWER TO THE UNIVERSE IS 42? BOLLOCKS IT'S 50

Having recently chalked up a half century chronologically, I have a way to go to get there mentally, I know within myself age is just a number. In life, we take numbers for granted, use them all of the time, and yet never ask "what exactly *is* a number?"

It's fascinating when you discover the number 2 for example is undefinable ... yes really. If you went searching for the number 2 where would you begin? Deepest Siberia... I think not! Numbers are a concept that we create mentally for the purpose of separating 'things'. Thus numbers aren't anything tangible, yet they are the same for everyone, everywhere.

With numbers being the *fundamental* principle of maths, does that mean everything can be explained mathematically? Some theoretical scientists believe so, but to do so they must omit something. That something is *consciousness!* It stands to reason if your theory has to omit anything then it cannot be fundamental. I mean how could it? At the source of all, the fundamental level, everything must be accounted for. Anything that you become 'aware of' must 'be'. It's like the kid in the playground who has been ostracised from the group. They might not be wanted, but they still exist. Ask yourself "am I conscious? Am I aware of something? Am I aware that I am aware?" I imagine you all answered yes to each of the questions. Ok good, so let me put it another way, would you also agree with the statement - *I am* aware that *I am* aware? Once again I'm sure the answer is yes, so how many remember the story of Moses and the burning bush? Moses asked "Who are you?" and the response from the big fella was "*I am* that *I am*". Do you notice the connection Sherlock?

To solve the mystery to life you must first see the pattern

The bible, a collection of books by various authors, spanning many hundreds of years was hi-jacked by a Roman emperor who made it the core of a religion. It is in essence, for the most part, a spiritual not religious guide for *all* when read in the right context. That context, I believe, is from a consciousness point of view containing hidden meaning, with the stories not to be taken literally. The Ark, the Holy Grail, even Jesus are all metaphors. Jesus tells us "I am the way, the truth and the life", "I am the light of the world", "I am the bread of life", "I am the gate", all metaphors; for when *you* accept the 'I am' statement you lay claim to what you believe to be true, projecting outwardly your inner power of creation.

Getting back to numbers... riveted huh! Numbers are based on set theory which to understand the number 2 we mentally construct two invisible boxes surrounding two 'things' within a single box referred to as a set which we '*consciously*' denote as a *set* of two. At the root of set theory is the empty set. With mathematics based on numbers and numbers based on the empty set then it stands to reason that all of mathematics springs from the empty set. What is the empty set? The empty set is *nothing* or better put *no-thing in particular. No-thing in particular* must have a *potential* to be something. Hence the empty set is the 'potential to be'. The Buddha espoused that reality springs from the void of infinite potential - the empty set, hence could consciousness at its root be the potential to be?

Modern cosmology is slowly catching up, with the realisation, that black holes (voids of infinite potential with a singularity at their core) are *not* the most destructive forces in the universe, but actually might be the most creative. It is in all likelihood that stars and galaxies are created by black holes and by taking a quantum leap so is everything in existence – including you and me. Could it be that we are all the production of black hole dynamics. Look up on a clear night and what do you see? The light from distant stars and galaxies. If we take away this light what are we left with? Nothing! There would be total darkness – a void! Is it possible that our universe could be a giant black hole with us acting as the singularity, observing itself from the inside? Enlightened? Maybe not yet! Stick with it - all roads lead home *eventually*.

CAN I HAVE SECONDS PLEASE?

On my second visit to the coffee shop, while drinking my coffee with Karen as she was plugged into her sleek new iPhone in truly modern fashion, I was plugged into gazing at the sleek young waitress. I noted how her attractive, symmetrical features gave her that 'pretty' girl look. Guys will know what I mean.

There are girls who are attractive, but not necessarily good looking. There are girls who are good looking but not pretty and then there are girls who just make you melt. This girl's a melter!... maybe not the best choice of phraseology. A melter where I come from is a slang term for someone who would literally do your head in. Maybe she would! Time might tell, it's a terrible... anyway.

I must admit I couldn't help but stare a little, catching her eye on one particular occasion, but trying not to seem weird or anything like that. There was something so enigmatic about her. It was not only her looks topped with the awesome purple hair that caught my attention, but also her mannerisms and the way she engaged with the customers. She conducted herself in a manner more befitting the owner than a waitress. Maybe she is I thought.

My mind wandered. I wonder what her name is. I have a silly habit of giving people nicknames when talking with Karen. I do this a lot with my clients. Over the years Tommy was affectionately known as Tommy Tucker the little f***...ella. Don't get the wrong impression, Tommy was one of the most amazing blokes I ever met, short on stature, but big on presence who had a massive impact on me. It's just my stupid sense of humour. My mum used to always say "John your sense of humour will get you into trouble". Mums are usually right! I miss Tommy, he passed away a few years back. Then there is Hector, known as hectic mainly due to his terrible time keeping. Colin was collywobbles as he was anything but! Hilary - Hillbilly Bentley, I've absolutely no idea! Norma – Normski, Samina – Semolina, Suresh – Sir Reg Empy (local politician) mainly due to Norma not being able to pronounce his name properly, Alison (Ali) was Ali Baba extrapolated to Ali Babaliscious on her hot days and the list goes on. Not knowing the name of the new object of my attention, I say this loosely... honestly as I had little to work with, I associated her to the girls with the purple wigs in the 70s t.v. series. I would think of her as my U.F.O. (Unidentified female object).

Although I'm reasonably comfortable with ageing, or so I thought, it slowly dawned on me the potential age difference. Not that it really mattered, but what age did I think my UFO might be? Mid to late twenties was my guess. It was then that I started to feel all of my fifty years again. So much for that bloody empty set! Why suddenly then? I'm not quite sure. I can hear all of you in unison "we know why!!!"

IT'S MY PARTY AND I'LL CRY IF I WANT TO

We all want to be the young good looking hero in the story we tell ourselves throughout our lifetime. Most of the time this is obviously not the case, but we can dream! It's our story and we have the free will to tell it from whatever perceptible point of view we choose.

Try this... take the time during the course of the day and listen to your 'self-talk', the little voice in your head that chirps away in the background that most of us never confront. Actually... who the heck is it? When you think about it, you have the ability to observe this little voice. If we can observe it, are we the voice or are we the observer? Jesus! Could there be two of me? I can hear Karen now, please God no! Christ! was that an observation or did the little voice say that? For all my Christian friends there's your *holy* trinity! If it upsets anyone please don't blame me, it was the little voice... I think.

When you take the time to observe your 'inner voice' it will dawn on you how much control it has over your life. This voice is an amalgamation of all the voices from all the people you have ever had contact with which includes the written word and the media. You may think it is solely yours, but it is not. This voice is correlated with the sub-conscious programmes that run constantly in the background which control your life – for the most part anyway. This makes it easier for you to focus on the things you enjoy and also the things you do not. It allows the conscious mind to navigate to destinations of your choice whilst filling in the blanks and catering for the mundane. Optimally the sub-conscious mind applies the scenery to your story, both foreground and background, allowing the conscious mind to navigate whilst telling the story, but for most people, a lot of the time, this isn't the case.

The story you tell yourself is pivotal to your life – it is your life. We have been brainwashed into believing life happens to us; that we have very little control over the people, places, circumstances and events that we engage with on a daily basis. Let me enlighten those who hold this belief. This could not be further from the truth. *You* are the illuminating power behind the people, places, circumstances and events in your life; it is all a co-creation that you are very much a part of. You have chosen everyone and everything that you have ever experienced out of life's great library. The ancients referred to it as the Akashic records. In modern scientific parlance it is known as the zero-point field or vacuum density where *all* information *ever* is stored or more accurately accessed. You have also chosen how you have felt in any given moment and added your interpretation to those experiences which you then feedback for the purpose of creating the next experience ad infinitum. This process of choosing - experiencing - interpreting all happens simultaneously, yet paradoxically you experience it on a moment to moment basis.

This process can also be seen as retro-causal action (backward causation) – the future somehow influencing what is experienced now. It's all related to the perspective taken. From your biological perspective, it appears it's only the past which influences the present moment (cause followed by effect) but in reality from your spiritual perspective it's actually an *entanglement* of a future event and a past event (which from your spiritual self's higher perspective doesn't exist on a timeline) all happening in the one eternal moment to create an experience *now*.

> *"The distinction between the past, present and future is only a stubbornly persistent one".*
>
> Albert Einstein

When viewed this way it is not too outlandish to reason that you have the power to change the past or more accurately your perceived past. You see there is only *the one* eternal moment of now. Everything that we experience *ever* is in the *now* and when you *accept* that life is paradoxically based on experiences and the feedback of said experiences, the penny hopefully starts to drop.

> *"We are not human beings having a spiritual experience. We are spiritual beings having a human experience."*
>
> Pierre Teilhard de Chardin

THE DUALITY OF TIME

I am not knocking our notion of time and saying it doesn't exist. What I am saying is it only appears to exist from your biological point of view and is obligatory for the purpose of separating experiences to tell your unique story. We all perceive the passage of time differently. When you are having fun, time flies, when you're not, it can drag. It is also entangled with memory, because if you lose both your short and long term memories then no time will appear to have passed from your point of view. Its direct opposite eternity underpins time and with this realisation it affords you the knowledge that everything is possible. Achieving is a different ball game, but we'll come to that. Another aspect of time is its dual nature. Remember everything experienced in the external world is of dual nature.

1) **Time Is Memory Experienced** – this is the internal experience of time.
2) **Time Is Movement Experienced** – this is the external experience measured by the movement of celestial objects.

FUNDAMENTAL FEEDBACK SOLUTION... FFS

It is important to understand what I mean by feedback. Let me give you an example. It has been calculated that a Rubix cube has around 43 quintillion possible permutations – what sort of number *is* that??? It has also been calculated that if one move per second was taken it could take a blind man, with *no* feedback of information, longer to complete than the predicted duration of the known Universe. Now *with* a feedback stream of information allowing the system to evolve (with the system being you as the subject entangled with the cube as the object) the cube can be completed in 20 moves. That, my friend, shows the potential of your true inner power. At the fundamental level, feedback is the universe experiencing itself through you, with you co-creating the experience along with the universe (collective consciousness).

My son Jordan completing a Rubix cube in under two minutes (using feedback)

IMAGINE THE CAUSE –
EXPERIENCE THE EFFECT

A word on quantum entanglement. A feedback loop is a tangled hierarchical system or is it an entangled hierarchical system? Why does this matter? It matters a great deal because when viewed from the higher perspective it shows everything must be based on oneness with the other a delusion of the mind. I could have said illusion instead of delusion, but delusion is more accurate as it is the mind which deludes itself into believing the illusion. Let's look at the difference in meaning between tangled and entangled. To begin with, tangled is a noun with entangled being a verb – a doing word.

Entangled – is almost always used when one thing becomes entwined with something else due to cause and effect.

Tangled – the levels of causality are so intertwined that we no longer can identify which is the cause and which is the effect.

Mainstream science likes cause and effect. It is easier to logically comprehend and requires no special entity. The sun rises as does the temperature, the sun sets and the temperature drops this is a simple entangled hierarchy of the sun being the cause with temperature variation being the effect. This is how external reality appears to work.

Towards the end of the nineteenth century, all appeared grand in physics, then the quantum realm was discovered. What was all the fuss about? This microscopic internal domain tossed everything on its head. The realisation that all matter, including you and me, is composed of tiny little building blocks of sub-atomic particles that do not obey any of the physical external reality laws. In fact they appeared to be the direct opposite. Instead of matter being composed of tiny solid 'things' it was discovered it was made from energy oscillating at different frequencies connected by some force – nothing solid. Further experimentation revealed that 'physical' objects in the macroscopic world of our experience required an observer (you and me) to put it there and that, what was being observed, was underpinned by probability waves – a probability wave is the likelihood for the *potential* to be. No observer, nothing definite – in other words whatever reality is, it requires an observation to come into being. This of course throws up a paradox. Who or what is observing *you* the observer?

> *"All matter originates and exists only by virtue of a force... We must assume behind this force the existence of a conscious and intelligent Mind. This mind is the matrix of all matter."*

> *Max Planck (The father of quantum physics)*

Quantum physics is the fundamental theory of nature at the smallest scales of energy levels of atoms and subatomic particles. I believe quantum entanglement connected to the observer to be *the* biggest player in the quantum world. Experimental evidence of an entangled pair of subatomic particles separated by the width of the observable universe suggests that when the polarisation or spin of one particle is observed the other exhibits the opposite polarisation or spin instantaneously. This involves faster than light speed communication, which upset Einstein deeply. The significance of this is profound. This has been tested time and time again and shows, whether you allow yourself to accept it or not, (it's up to you) that a higher power must be at play!

In the classical world in which we live, information cannot travel faster than the speed of light. This is not the case in the quantum realm. So what gives? It is due to what's known as non-locality. Non-locality simply means, no separate objects or 'things' exist at any particular time at the quantum scale; everything is connected as one, like a spread out wave. Yet we experience a classical world where things or objects are separated by defined locations at particular *times*, but remember this is always from our own personal observation or point of view. To fully comprehend the quantum realm you must accept the opposite to be true; that no *time* or *separation* exists, with everything being connected simultaneously as feedback loops – a *tangled* rather than *entangled* hierarchy. Instead of linearity (straight lines) existing between two points, which is our common understanding, it is really the hidden fractal geometry of spin and angular momentum that underpins reality. The quantum world cannot be physicalised; it is more akin to an *activity* of *abstract* ideas which reveals itself, in a physical sense, through geometrical spirals and mathematical probabilities. So what springs to '*mind*' (excuse the pun) that you possess or have access to that is an activity of abstract ideas?

We are all aware that time appears to speed up or slow down depending on our mood. An experience *always* happens in the present moment. For a new experience to be had, a perceived future and perceived past event must merge together in the moment of now. Think about it - this imagined future and imagined past can only exist 'now'. Now is all there is. It is all based on a singular feedback loop, which is paradoxically infinite (embedded fractally), of *imagined* future events and an *imagined* past circumstances all creating the experiences of now. *Imagination* is what drives the whole system of *infinity*. Einstein slowly came to realise this when developing his theory of relativity.

He also showed how the stand alone concept of time does not exist. Hence, he amalgamated space and time proposing the singular concept of spacetime, with this spacetime concept being a continuum. A continuum is defined as, a continuous sequence in which adjacent elements are not perceptibly different from each other, but the extremes are quite distinct. Sounds exactly like an entangled quantum system, which you are continuously constructing mentally. Or to be more accurate, as discussed previously, a *tangled* hierarchical feedback loop system of your own doing.

> *"Size is not a reality, but a construct of the mind; and space a construct to contain constructs"*
>
> Robert Anton Wilson

This concept of spacetime was a quantum leap from the Newtonian mechanical clockwork universe where it was thought a universal clock kept a record. But spacetime ran into its own problems. It shed light on the fact that the events in your life that appear to happen one after the other, constructing a linear time line of your life, is not the case. In fact, spacetime revealed that each moment experienced did not necessarily precede the previous experience. Weird or what! In other words, there is no true sequence to the events of your life from a spacetime perspective. For spacetime to work, to overcome this incredible hurdle, Einstein and his mathematicians had to accept that there must be an infinity of spacetimes. Going somewhat deeper, spacetime is really another term for causality with causality being the relationship between cause and effect from your perspective. It is the effect of the cause from *each* observer's perspective which never completely agree. The implications of this are staggering. It suggests there are infinite versions of you, not just the singular you that you believe yourself to be in this lifetime. Cool or what!

Fundamentally for spacetime to work, the duality of *space* and *time* had to merge as a singularity with all singularity's being infinite. Hence an infinity of spacetimes or causalities or singularities exist – take your pick. Everything comes from and is *one* anyway. Anything perceived as fundamental must become *one* which is *infinite* from the biological perspective or it cannot be fundamental. One and infinity are the same anyway. But the 'one' can turn up in many different guises with *spacetime* being just one example. Infinite versions of self provide the same outcome. Parallel universes related to the multiverse theory also ends up with infinity and the one multiverse. Religion believes in the *One* true God, dependent on which variant you choose, which once again is believed to be infinite and eternal. All roads home lead to the singularity (oneness) which is itself infinite and eternal.

Revelations of this nature strengthened my belief that when Robyn died it was only in the story I was telling myself. Life is composed of infinite stories therefore there are many stories where Robyn is alive, well and healthy. What I need to do is change my back story, to a version that not so much brings us back together because in truth we have never been apart, but quantum leap to a different perspective. Believe me, this takes a while to get your head around.

COLOUR CO-ORDINATED

With my job as a Personal Trainer I tend to have numerous chunks of free time throughout the day. It's part of the job. People turn up late or on occasions have to cancel, hence time for coffee. When Jordan was about ten years old and Robyn six, they would joke that daddy's job was counting to ten and drinking coffee. A highly accurate summation some would say! To be fair though, being a Personal Trainer is not just about motivating people to exercise and taking them through a personalised programme, you also need to be a good listener and on occasions, counsellor. Developing a rapport with your clients is essential. It helps if you can make them laugh or at the very least that they find you somewhat amusing and interesting. My colleague Michael has definitely nailed this! To be a top Personal Trainer you also need good business acumen so it really is a multifaceted profession.

There are worse jobs. I graduated as a mechanical engineer and began work in the C.I.D. of a large aerospace company. Sounds interesting? Not really. The Colouring In Department as we were known, was all about recording man hours spent in production and colouring in bars on charts for the purpose of producing graphs for the accountants to cost the jobs. For me it was not the most fulfilling of work. I needed more.

About six weeks into the job, I was on a training course which provided the new recruits with a company wide overview when I had my epiphany. Standing in an old dank workshop, in the middle of winter that hadn't been used for quite some time, I noticed a calendar in the corner. It had a picture of what looked to me like a Caribbean beach scene. Surrounded by the grey back drop, the colours in the calendar appeared so vibrant. It was there and then that I thought I must do something more colourful with my life. This was the first occasion that a contrast in colour had such an impact on me. It took me another five years before my hobby became my profession. Looking back, I can see how my dreams became my reality. Bear in mind, at the time there were only a few Personal Trainers in the country, with the industry being very much in its infancy. Personal Training was not as embedded in the societal psyche as it is today.

My point being, many of us go through the daily grind hating what we do to make ends meet. It doesn't have to be that way. In a more subtle way, it is something you have chosen to accept; dragging yourself out of bed at the scrake of dawn, to go to a place you end up dreading and spending one third of your day doing something you have grown to hate. This is what many of us call living. You were not born to work. It's society that dictates you do, so why not choose something you like. A job that lights up your day and brightens your outlook. It's your choice.

LET'S DANCE

For my dream of finding Robyn to become reality, I had to journey down the rabbit hole to discover fundamental truths. I needed to know who we really are and where did we come from? I wanted to know the purpose to life; I wanted to know my purpose. I also intuitively knew, if I was able to find the answers to these questions, it would also provide the answer to where we go when we die. As I'm sure you can imagine, this journey goes deep, way beyond consensual reality. My first book 'The Yo(u)niverse Paradox' goes into great detail in this subject. Due to this I will simplify as best I can and keep it brief, so stick with it... it's enlightening!

Many people are waking up to the realisation that life is primarily a biological system and not a physical one (which is currently the modern scientific viewpoint). Even the scientific community are realising this, but are still slow to acknowledge and believe me *they are slow*. A paradigm shift usually only occurs when the old guard die to allow the new to flourish. In fact, for the scientific community to avoid the inevitable - that the world is created via biology and not physics – they are now proposing that we are living in a computer generated simulation. We are not! The latest research has shown the energy required for this is unfathomable.

This might surprise some people, but for the most part, the current western paradigm still insists that we are unconscious robots meandering through a chaotic, random world, with little or no control of our thoughts, feelings and actions. Really? For this to be the case, some 'higher power', but don't mention God, heavens above! jeez erase that too, is pulling the strings by writing the programmes of our existence. J e s u s C h r i s t! When's the second coming??? And I'm not even religious! Anyway his second name's not Christ! Christ is a reference to the Christ consciousness he demonstrated and that exists within all of us. I do feel sorry for those who take messages literally and I'll let you into a little secret... he's not coming back. I mean, come back from where? Come back from when? You see, everything exists only in the present moment in *your* mind constructed from *your* point of view and that includes Jesus, the Buddha, even Roger Daltry. It's *you* who creates the where, the when and The Who! People try to put us d-down (talking about my generation)... to be fair if you want to believe Roger is making a comeback or Jesus *is* coming back it's your divine right, but the meaning is lost *in* you. The teachings of Jesus are allegories of *your* divine conscious potential. When Jesus said things like, "You can do as I do and more" and "I and the father are one and so are you", he is referencing the Christ divinity in *you*. If I am correct and I know I am - what a responsibility *you* have. You co-create with every other aspect of consciousness (all that is), but you must accept that everything that has ever happened to you, is happening right now or is going to happen to you in the future *from your point of view* is your creation. Yes... *your* creation.

31

"Everything we hear is an opinion, not a fact. Everything that we see is a perspective, not the truth."

Marcus Aurelius

What appears to you as a fact only arises from your own point of view. Hence it can only be your opinion about something, even if the general consensus is in agreement. The general consensus of others is still arising from your perspective, therefore there are no universal facts – just opinions. This understanding about reality is crucial. It is the realisation that from your perspective, you are the creator of your own unique reality tunnel. Everybody and everything that comes into your reality tunnel is a reflection of you, put there by you, for the purpose of experience through you. In each moment, all that you ever do, is create an experience. There is nothing else for you to do. You create joyful experiences, you create sad experiences, you also create death and destruction, but most of the time you create habits which are repeating programmes run by your sub-conscious mind that define your ego self. The ego, is the false illusion of who we think we are, which is enhanced by the feedback we receive from others.

Life is a conscious perpetual feedback loop co-creating from two perspectives; yours and paradoxically everyone/everything else's (collective consciousness). You create life with life creating you. The world you create blinks in and out of existence at the speed of light. It is actually in the 'off' position as much as the 'on'. You only see it as the 'on' continuum due to the relatively slow speed your brain processes the frames of reference. It's due to this slowing down of frames of reference that we can thread together a story, but that's a story for another day. Why a co-creation? As the saying goes it takes two to tango!

TANGERINES ANYONE?

Every hero has an anti hero or antagonist. Everything at the fundamental level has its opposite. You have positive and negative, matter and antimatter, up and down, male and female, in and out, open and closed, tangerine and... um hold on, give me a minute... ummm, oh yes! I did say at the fundamental level. As you expand beyond fundamental scales you create an infinity of expression. As you can imagine, it is easy to get lost in the mire of infinity due to the complexity that arises. Opposites then become more vague as so many different perspectives can be taken. Take an elephant. What's the opposite of an elephant? The first thing that springs to mind for most is a mouse, but why? By power of association - an elephant is large and a mouse small. Does that make them opposites? No, but from one perspective it pushes them closer to opposite ends of the spectrum.

The more diverse the universe becomes, the greater the complexity, the more variables that have to be accounted for. To quote Wikipedia – (Complexity theory is an interdisciplinary theory that grew out of systems theory in the 1960's. It draws from research in the **natural** sciences that examines **uncertainty** and **non-linearity**. Complexity theory emphasises interactions and the accompanying **feedback loops** that **constantly change** systems. While it proposes that systems are unpredictable, they are also **constrained by order generating rules**). Before I had ever heard of complex theory, I wrote about what I believe to be the fundamental pattern that would appear to govern complex theory, in my first book The Yo(u)niverse Paradox. This explained the tangled hierarchy (feedback loop) of opposites and how they're embedded fractally. Modern scientific parlance refers to this as quantum entanglement.

THE SECRET IS ATTRACTION

A lot of you might have heard of The Secret, an excellent book/ movie revealing the law of attraction and how you can use this to empower yourself to live the life of your dreams. The law of attraction is simply like attracts like. How you feel on the inside (different feelings vibrate at different frequencies) attracts the matching vibration (experiences) you have on the outside. Now I'm sure you are all well aware of the saying "opposites attract". This being the case then how does like attract like? It's about perspective – this power of creation is always from your point of view.

"Human beings do not attract what they
want – they attract who they are"

Dr. Wayne Dyer

Take two magnets and bring them close together. If the north pole of one is in alignment with the south pole of the other they will attract, but if you align the north poles of both or the south poles of both you will experience repulsion. In this case, opposite poles attract not like poles. Why? Because from your point of view both magnets exist in the outer boundary condition the 'outside world'. The law of attraction states like attracts like, but from the inside out. A boundary condition must be crossed to define inside and outside. What is this boundary condition? This boundary condition is you. It's you, from your biological perspective. Biology is the interface between the inner world of thoughts and feelings (the quantum/spiritual realm) and the classical outer realm of illusory *experiences* of solidity and separation.

To recap: You are the boundary condition and when it's crossed it's like attracts like. When the boundary condition is not crossed for the most part it's opposites attract, but with the caveat that nothing is one hundred percent – there are no absolute facts! In quantum terms this is Heisenberg's uncertainty principle – the more you know about the velocity of a sub-atomic particle the less you know about where it is and if you happen to know where it is you will have absolutely no idea it's speed and where it's going! In layman's terms this is change. *Nothing* stays the same – *everything* changes, with it all being generated through the law of opposites.

1,2,3... INFINITY

You exist in a world of duality with everything *being* constructed by the power of three – the fabled holy trinity, but it makes more sense when spelt wholly trinity. Why? With consciousness 'all that is' being *whole* and complete upon itself for the purpose of experience, it requires a system to express and engage with itself that is a sub-set of wholeness (a fractal). Religious zealots love to hijack a term and try to give it a definite meaning. From the Christian perspective the holy trinity is - the Father, Son and Holy Ghost. This is only one version of *a wholly* trinity. *The* wholly trinity is the power of three which is fundamental to the evolution of everything. It is based on how Wholeness - God – 'all that is' (your choice) not only divides but expresses itself for the purpose of creation. Hence the wholly trinity is not a single unique triumvirate, it is all of them; it is *the* process of creation.

The wholly trinity is the expression of two extremes (duality) with an infinity of expressions in between. Here are a few examples - an electric current always manifests a magnetic field and a magnetic field always generates an electric current with both expressing the electromagnetic spectrum. Black and white are considered opposites with both connected by infinite shades of grey similar to light and dark connected by an infinite spectrum of luminosity. In other words, infinity resides between opposites or complementary systems.

At the fundamental or ground state of existence there is only *One* or *Nothing* dependent on your perspective. *One* can be expressed as a singularity, unity, wholeness, infinity or 'all that is'. *Nothing* (no-thing in particular) can be expressed as potential: the potential to be. It's bloody confusing I know, but *one* what? The *potential to be* what? The answer... whatever *you* choose.

THE FANTASTIC VOYAGE

I remember when I was a kid growing up being enthralled watching a movie about the U.S. Government having developed the ability to miniaturise matter by shrinking individual atoms for a short period of time. They used the technology to attempt to save a dying mans life by shrinking a submarine and a number of crew members and injecting them into his body. They were tasked with releasing a blood clot in the man's brain, but only have about sixty minutes before they slowly start returning to normal size.

Like every adventure story they battled the elements, in this case it was the man's heart, lungs and various immune system responses as well as the token saboteur. The idea of the sub-atomic realm held a fascination with me then as it does now. It is in this realm where you begin to find the answers to what reality really is.

THEY SEEK HIM HERE, THEY SEEK HIM THERE, THEY SEEK HIM EVERY F**KING WHERE!

It's not only Joe public, but the mainstream scientific community are still blinded by the concept of mind. I find it funny that a lot of the people who receive funding for researching the mind-brain connection, and are tasked with informing the rest of us Joe's, can't see the wood for the trees. I understand attempting to define what the mind *is* can be very tricky, but surely after all this time you would think something so prominent would be better understood. It helps when you realise ... you are what you seek!

Is the mind and the brain the same thing? Absolutely not. Are they correlated? Absolutely. How? Firstly they exist in different dimensions, sort of. It's this dimensional rationale that creates controversy and mixes things up. Think of it this way. The brain is a noun with mind being a verb. The brain is an organ, an actual 'thing' that can be labelled, whereas mind cannot be labelled as such and is continually 'doing'. Think of mind as an activity; as perpetual motion.

The brain on the other hand is an organ housed within most living beings. I say most because there are some living organisms that do not have a brain, at least not in the traditional sense, but still function at a very limited degree. The outer layer of these particular organisms, the part that engages with their outside environment, acts as their brain, much like the cells that make up your body. Ironically the outer skin of a cell, which cellular biologist Bruce Lipton demonstrated, *is* the brain of the cell called the membrane. The membrane, like a regular brain, acts as a transmitter/receiver of information between the cell itself and its outside environment.

The mainstream educational system still proposes that the nucleus of the cell is the control centre ... the brain. This perpetuates the belief that we are all victims of our genes. In actuality, the nucleus of the cell acts as the gonad... the reproduction system. It stores the blueprints to replace broken down proteins to maintain normal cellular function. If the nucleus of the cell was the brain then the expectation of it being removed would be cellular death. This is not the case, the cell continues to function normally. It will eventually die due to proteins breaking down and not being replaced. The belief that we are victims of our genes is very much an outdated belief that still lingers in the collective psyche. The belief that if a cancer gene exists in the family there isn't a whole lot you can do about it, outside of a few lifestyle changes, is utter nonsense.

"If you think you can, or you think you can't, you are right."

Henry Ford

None of us are victims of our genes, but we can choose to be. Yes... we are dealt a hand at birth with our genes being passed down from our parents, but due to every gene having an epigene (a switch) we have the ability to turn the genes off and on. Epigenes are controlled by the perceptions we have of our environment (reality tunnel) that we engage with and the beliefs we hold.

I am sure we have all heard of the placebo effect. The effect produced by a perception or belief that a positive outcome will be gained. This means, no matter what you put your faith in, if you believe strongly enough you will attain a positive outcome. That being the case, then how come we don't always achieve a positive outcome? The reason for this is the little known nocebo effect. If you have been following the thread thus far I'm sure you can guess the nocebo effect is the opposite to the placebo. It is the perception or belief of a negative outcome. Life evolves from the ebb and flow of the most likely outcome arising from the strength of our positive thoughts and feelings wedded to the strength of our negative thoughts and feelings about any given situation or circumstance. As you can imagine this process can be very complex which allows for the infinite diversity of our collective experiences. The brain is involved in this process, but is superseded by mind.

"What you think, you become. What you feel, you attract. What you imagine, you create."

Buddha

We can see the brain, but we cannot see mind. The brain is an electrical switching station, it does not think. The brain has never conjured a thought, ever. It is a transmitter/receiver of information which I believe is holographic in nature, projecting an external mental hologram that you perceive as your reality. This can be best explained via the holofractographic theory, simply put, a holographic theory wedded to fractal geometry which I discuss in detail in The Yo(u)niverse Paradox.

Many people conclude that by looking at an MRI scan where a particular region of the brain lights up, when people think of 'whatever', is proof the brain is thinking. This is like saying a footprint in the sand is a foot. What you are seeing in a particular region of the brain is the electrical switches firing when thoughts are activated. That is very different to a root thought. The big question then is, who is *being* the activator, *doing* the activating and *having* the activation?

Let's first take a step back and turn our attention inward towards mind. The statement 'you are what you seek' is the key to understanding mind. Think about it. We are using mind to ask the question what is mind. This is paradoxical. A paradox is a mental feedback loop that basically gets stuck in a continuous loop with no resolution. The most well known probably being "What came first, the chicken or the egg?" It is well documented that a problem cannot be resolved at the level it is created. Therefore it is impossible from the level of mind to resolve paradoxes due to mind being the cause and source. This implies when you ask at the fundamental level, what came first, is and always will be unanswerable. There is no first or last, fundamentally time does not exist. I cannot stress enough how important it is to understand this. This being the case, we can conclude mind is not truly fundamental, but paradoxically is the fundamental expression of that which is. There must be an even greater power at the source of all... a power source.

In fact, we will shortly see how you can shut mind down and are still aware. Therefore it stands to reason that it must be this *awareness* which is primary. If *you* were not *aware*, your mind would eventually get stuck in a constant loop unable to do anything else. It would be perpetually stuck until the power runs out. This is exactly what happens when your computer freezes and gets stuck in a continuous loop. The computer has no awareness therefore is not aware it is stuck. It is you who gets pissed off not the computer! The computers not thinking "ah for fuck sake I'm chasing my tail again!" It just keeps going around in circles. Isn't it funny when we observe a dog chasing its tail. The dog's awareness is not at the level a human exhibits (well most anyway), but it is aware to some degree because it eventually stops, either through boredom or tiredness. Note: All biological systems exhibit some level of awareness, even those without a brain and we have all come across a few of them!

> *"Under certain circumstances, profanity provides*
> *a relief denied even to prayer."*
>
> *Mark Twain*

I just thought I would throw that in, just in case anyone gets offended by the power of swear words, especially in this ridiculously, politically correct environment we find ourselves socially engaging in, at the time of writing. Remember this, it is you and only you who always decides whether you are offended or not!

With that in mind let's get back to it. What are the implications of mind not being a 'thing' but an activity? Immense! Philosophically, activity is action. Action is defined as 'movement or change performed by an *agent'*. Let me repeat 'by an agent'. As we peel away the layers once again the truth reveals itself. The *agent* or *activator* activating activity (wholly trinity) cannot be labelled as such as it is also not a 'thing'. For any 'thing' to be labelled it must have boundaries. No boundaries – no label. Still as you are *aware* of the boundless you can conclude you must be an activity within this boundless awareness. You could say that you are an *individuation* (individual) from your point of view, of a collective absolute conscious awareness. This unnamable absolute conscious awareness just *'being'* (a little clue) is all individual conscious awareness's amalgamated as one unbounded entity. Ok I'll get to the *fecking* point... you are God observing yourself! You are observing, from a limited perspective, the amalgamation of all observers which simultaneously is observing you. It's a feedback loop.

Instead of using the term God as it doesn't sit well with many people, let's use the term 'all that is', as this implies a non religious entity. I've explained 'all that is' expresses itself by the power of three; the 'wholly' trinity. Christianity refers to it as Father, Son and Holy Ghost, but it is much more than that. It is really the triumvirate of mind and how it functions – with Father referencing the Sub-conscious mind, Son the conscious mind and The Holy Ghost the higher or supra conscious mind. The sub-conscious mind runs the background programmes that you are not focused on. The conscious mind activates when you focus your attention, with the higher consciousness *'being'* the observer of it all and connecting everything and every non-thing together – not only from your soul's perspective but the oversoul (amalgamation of all souls). Do you see the pattern. This is all from your point of view and everything from your point of view is always of dual nature. Your mind constructs meaning from two fundamentally opposing views with an infinity of possibilities-in-between. Later I will show in the outer world of our perceptions, via our sensory apparatus, how everything is connected by the space-in-between, which is really mentally this infinity of possibilities-in-between.

From all of this we can conclude that if mind is not a thing but an activity – a process - then the environment you perceive to *interact* with is primarily a mental construct and not a physical one that our senses have us believe. Many will say things like, "Drop a brick on your foot and tell me your metaphorical brick doesn't hurt your metaphorical foot". This is a lame argument. Why? Because it is based on the belief a material, solid world is fundamental because our senses tell us so. If our senses were correct then the earth is flat and static and the sun is the size of a coin. We are all aware our senses get stumped by the veil of truth. When you accept that we create the world through our personal belief system wedded to our sensory apparatus, which is based on electromagnetism, you can then welcome more readily the idea that the matrix is created mentally. With our personal belief system being heavily influenced by the general consensus, making us aware a brick is generally heavy, our sensory awareness will most likely leave us in no doubt! Yet this is not always the case, we do have dominion over what happens as we are the creators in the first place. When you take control and know without doubt that you will not get hurt you might discover the brick is a rubber prop, or it hits your foot, but for some strange reason it doesn't cause any pain. Stranger things happen. What I'm saying is, it doesn't require a massive leap of faith for what we believe to be material and solid is actually immaterial and a just mental picture we create to tell our personal story. In fact all the experimental data strongly backs this up. If you don't believe me, which is your divine right, go do the research.

When you mention to people the world is an illusion they look at you as if you have two heads, wondering which one's talking nonsense or in my case the most nonsense! Haha. I love it! I must say I am far from alone in my views. There are many scientists, philosophers and people just like you and me who have come to the same conclusions. Although as I mentioned earlier, instead of illusion, delusion is a better description, as it is the mind which deludes itself into believing the illusion to be real. This is why if you burst someone's world view bubble, they will quite often do everything in their power to patch it up rather than update their belief system. To move up the rungs of the spiritual ladder requires taking quantum leaps. If it didn't we would all realise who we truly are relatively quickly and end up telling pretty much the same story. With your true self wanting to experience all of its magnificence, this would be detrimental. It is interesting to note that the word detrimental has 'mental' in it. You might have noticed I use the word fundamental a lot! At the base level of reality – fundamentally – the term has the suffix mental (funda- **mental**). Ponder this - we don't say fundaphysical. Clues are often best hidden in plain sight.

When science at the beginning of the twentieth century developed the ability to peer into the quantum realm of atoms and sub-atomic particles they were staggered to find there was *nothing* there. "Hold on", they said, "surely that cannot be correct? The world has solid objects that we can see and touch so the world must be composed of very small particles because our sensory apparatus tells us so! If any non-qualified pleb says different, we will throw our toys out of the pram and inform them we are educated people with letters after our names. If any qualified person of similar ilk puts forth any absurd suggestions which challenges the long held mainstream view, we will laugh at them as they are flung to the farthest reaches of fringe science where no funding is forth coming and nobody pays any attention".

Ironically modern scientific wisdom has lagged way behind many indigenous cultures, who were well aware the world is a delusion created by mind, long ago. Why is it that the mainstream scientific community are so slow to accept new paradigms? Arrogance, ignorance and control of the masses springs to mind, quite often being profit driven! The scientific method is based on observation and measurement. Over time through repetition a statistical probability evolves, which if fits the current mode of thinking, becomes established. If it doesn't fit, it gets *ignored*. We are then fed a diatribe that accepted scientific knowledge is sacrosanct and not to be questioned. Bullshit! Science *is* all about questioning. Every 'thing' changes 'out there' in every moment, with small changes leading to big changes over time and that includes what was once considered established scientific fact.

> *"Knowledge is knowing a tomato is a fruit.*
> *Wisdom is not putting it in a fruit salad"*
>
> Miles Kington

Universally the only thing immune to change are the immutable laws that govern the pattern or process of life. This is why I keep harping on about fundamentals and why the scientific community will never be able to merge general relativity with quantum theory anytime soon because general relativity is not fundamental. When I started on my quest to discover the true nature of reality I inherently knew there was not much point in looking 'out there' at the infinite diversity of life. General relativity is the science of how large scale objects interact with each other in the universe at large. The predictions are very successful up to a point. Or to be more accurate the predictions are very accurate down to a point. That point is known as the singularity. The laws of general relativity fall apart and crumble when confronted with the singularity. The irony is the scientific community has never realised the singularity is the *observer* revealed in quantum theory. It is also the same observer alluded to throughout the aeons. This singularity is the observer of the universe. This universal observer is you, with the caveat, from your point of view. So all of this time it has been *You* who is the Scarlet Pimpernel!

IS IT A BIRD? IS IT A PLANE?
NO IT'S A COW!

To discover the fundamental base principles of creation you must look within yourself and into the quantum realm and the secrets it reveals.

Mind is limited and as I've shown not primary. Let's take an example. When you see a picture of a cow how do you know it's a cow? In reality, you don't. You see, as you were growing up, along the way you were shown a picture and told this is a cow, no doubt on more than one occasion. What if your parents had a wicked sense of humour and always referred to it as a cock. You go to school convinced what everyone else calls a cow is a cock... I'm referring to a rooster for crying out loud! But as far as you're concerned, it's everyone else who's the prick!

This provides us with a glimpse into the fundamental nature of linguistics. Just like the concept of numbers stems from the empty set which is nothing, the same can be said about linguistics. Linguistics arises from nothing, here's an example. Instead of getting into, what the rest of us call a car, you decide that it's your 'tool' you drive to work in. It's totally up to you; you can call it what you like. It's just everyone else who'll think you're the *tool*!

It is always *you* who decides on labels, but this is obviously impacted throughout your lifetime. Within your reality bubble, the only way you will change your mind and accept what others are telling you is generally two fold. By the power of numbers i.e. peer pressure or from a more respected source eg. a teacher.

Let's take it a little deeper. When you were a child you might have only ever seen a picture of a cow. Now I'm sure we can all agree a picture of a cow is not an actual living cow, but mind is so powerful that by the power of association when you see a cow for the first time in a field, say humping another cow, you somehow still know it's a cow. Hopefully at your tender years humping is another matter.

"Mum why's that cow got two heads?", "it's called duality son!"

And for any of you smart asses who know that a cow is female and that the male equivalent is a bull, it is still common practice for cows to mount other cows when they're going through oestrus. I wonder do some women go through ... well anyway where were we?

Your sub-conscious mind is conditioned throughout your lifetime, but most prevalently up to the age of seven. It continually downloads and records every person, place, circumstance and event that your sensory awareness brings you into contact with. In other words everything that has ever happened to you. Up to the age of seven, you are like a sponge absorbing everything with little conscious or critical thought involved. As you get older you begin to question more and develop the ability to discard certain information which you feel does not serve your story, whilst retaining strongly other information which serves as your belief system or world view. Between the ages of thirty five and forty two you generally reach your mental peak. For whatever reason, spiritual awakenings happen in roughly seven year cycles. During your forties, your spiritual awareness maximises and then there's fifty.

FIFTY NOT OUT

On the odd occasion whenever I do have a weakness about getting older, I always ask myself the question, how old am I if I don't know how old I am? This helps me deal with what is commonly termed middle age. Try it... ask yourself how old am I if I don't know how old I am? What's your answer? Put it on a postcard and send with a stamped address envelope to... that's a joke for you older folk! The younger generation are thinking wtf!

Thank god middle age is now considered fifty and not forty as it was back in the day. Still, this being the case, I'm not considered young anymore... fuck that! I still feel young. Then again who is it that decides the boundaries that we tend to perpetuate and live our lives by. I'm young, healthy and fit and that's that, at least until I see the look on people's faces when you tell them you remember, admittedly very vaguely, the moon landing hoax, sorry the moon landing... the way *mind* functions. Did they or didn't they? As the Shakespeare hoax, sorry Shakespeare, this is becoming a habit, tells us in Hamlet, "To be or not to be, that is the question".

I haven't celebrated my birthday since I turned forty. It was on the day of my forty first birthday when we got the devastating news that our daughter could be seriously ill. Robyn never got sick. I mean really, at least as far as my memory serves me. She was, is a real character; bright, determined and very funny. I would say to Robyn on a regular basis "you make me laugh".

This year I caved. I agreed to a fiftieth celebration so long as it wasn't near my official birthday. Turning fifty was not a big deal. I would be lying if I said it hadn't bothered me a little, but honestly not that much. Karen set it up as a surprise. I had never had a surprise party before although prior to leaving the house I thought maybe I should dress up a little. I had an inkling.

I sat on the bed and was transported back to Saturday January 6th 2007. On that evening I celebrated my fortieth birthday in a function room in the Four Winds restaurant/bar on the outskirts of Belfast. A client of mine, who was part owner, kindly supplied the room free of charge. A large gathering of family and friends made for a fantastic experience. I got up and did a short speech thanking all for coming. I was so pleased my mum was able to make it as her health had been deteriorating. I was also especially proud that both Jordan and Robyn were able to attend. They had a great night with Robyn getting in on the act to help me cut the cake.

Karen's father, Billy Hollywood (that's his real name) provided the entertainment. He's a one man band! Remember back in the day when the guy strapped the bass drum to his back with the drumstick attached via a cord to his stamping foot, cymbals between his thighs, a harmonica braced in front of his lips and playing the banjo all at the same time? Well, Bill played the guitar along side a backing tape! Bill's claim to fame was an appearance on Opportunity Knocks. The show that gave us the clapometer, with Hughie Green as the original Simon Cowell. Bill was playing lead guitar in the band; Barry Brent and the Jetset. I believe they came second to Lena Zavaroni or was it Peters and Lee?

IT'S ALL ABOUT PERSPECTIVE

Sitting on the bed a decade later I find myself welling up. The emotions come flooding back of how my life has changed so much from that wonderful night. My mum and Robyn have moved on to other worlds. In that moment I felt somewhat of a failure. I had made Robyn a promise, a promise to myself that we would always be together for ever and ever. That I would never let her go. I feel her presence all of the time. I very rarely visit her grave. It's not far from where we live, but I know in my heart that she is not really there. What I have come to realise is, Robyn is everywhere and nowhere all at the same time. This is our quantum essence. Everywhere and nowhere are actually *one* and the same. You can think of nowhere as now-here, so if Robyn's always in the here and now then by default she must be everywhere. Granted, this is not how we perceive the world. This is the omnipresence of 'all that is' your true self.

From the biological point of view, it would appear that we exhibit freewill. Although there is still a lot of conjecture surrounding whether or not our fate is predetermined or if we really do have choice. When you can accept that reality itself *is* infinite potential – the potential in each moment to be - with you being an aspect of this infinite potential empowered by the power of choice, you begin to realise that in a dualistic nature the answer is both and neither. Very Zen I know, but this is also what quantum physics espouses. Yes, no and maybe. It is the mental boundaries you have chosen to construct to live your life by that restricts your freewill. This all takes place in a spacetime mental mosaic unique to you and created by you, but paradoxically also everyone and everything else you choose to come into contact with. Take your time to contemplate this. It is quite profound. Who you truly are is not in space and time; you are that which experiences space and time – all of it. You are *also* the creator of your own spacetime reality tunnel feeding back your experience of it. This is your dual nature.

I am a firm believer that non existence is impossible. Try to think what it would be like to not exist. You can't! You always end up thinking of something. When you think you create – I think therefore I am – that's a little Renee Descartes number.

Ah! But what happens when you stop thinking I hear you cry! Is it possible to suppress your thoughts and stop thinking? The answer is yes.

From your perspective there are three main ways you can do this. The first is through observation without judgement. Take a moment to slowly look around your surroundings and as you do so do not define or label anything. Give it a try. When you do this properly you are actually not thinking, just observing.

The second is through techniques such as mindfulness or meditation. When you perform any of these techniques you slow down your brainwave patterns to alpha, theta and delta states. Our waking conscious state mostly functions at the beta level. This is when we are focusing our attention, performing everyday tasks and are alert to our surroundings. When we relax our thoughts and become calm, our brainwaves slow down and we become more connected to the present moment. This happens at the alpha level and is the beginning of mindfulness and the meditative state. The next level down is the theta state which occurs most often in sleep and deep meditation. When meditating in the theta state, our senses go inward and our external awareness is reduced dramatically. This is where we can influence change and redirect it to where *we* want to go. This is a great method we can use to allow our heart's desires to flow more freely into our reality tunnel.

When in dreamless sleep we enter the delta region where our external awareness of our surroundings shuts down. This is the third way we enter the state of no thought. The connection to body awareness has gone. The body is a vessel you construct through your conscious awareness of it, powered by the sub-conscious. Let me repeat, the real you is *not* your body!

Those who achieve a meditative state at the delta level have absolutely no doubt about this and create experiences far beyond their wildest dreams. They go to places that we cannot put into words. Language can be so restrictive. Some forty percent of those who have encountered a near death experience can also attest to this. Psychedelics such as DMT and ayahuasca have also taken people to dimensions far beyond this world and appear much more vivid and real than the daily dream we construct.

Last but not least are gamma waves which are the fastest brainwave frequencies that exist at a higher level to beta with all the rest existing lower. When you enter this state you may turn a shade of green and hulk out. Sorry, lame joke. Even though gamma waves resonate at a faster rate than the waking state of beta, mind still must be quiet to access. Researchers have discovered when in this range you associate with universal love, altruism and the 'higher virtues'. I believe you also enter this range when you are in the zone. The times in your life when you just know! You connect with your 'higher self' and expand. You become one; the whole universe.

It's interesting to note, the higher you go, the lower you go. As above, so below. This is the spiritual you. There is no 'up' or 'down' due to spirit existing everywhere and from this perspective no reference point is required. Everything expands spirally outwards whilst simultaneously curving back in on itself in an infinitely evolving geometrical pattern.

Let me provide a practical, real life example. A man is lost in a vast, flat desert. No matter where he looks he sees no reference points, not even the sun. Ok it's a desert, so in this case some artistic licence is required. Let's put the desert in Northern Ireland under a blanket of cloud. His guardian angel points him in the direction to safety. "Just keep walking straight as far as the eye can see and you will eventually come to an oasis". The man sets off determined to walk in a straight line happy in the knowledge he was born lucky – with both legs the same length. What could go wrong! His guardian angel observes from above and witnesses the man walking in an arc, which after a long enough period of time will curve back in on itself. Why is this? It is because straight lines do not really exist. You see everything spins, everything has angular momentum, and everything is in a constant state of flux. This goes all the way down to the smallest scale measurable; the Planck length. What we perceive as a straight line is only from our limited biological perspective. When we gaze at the stars we do not see the light shine back in a straight line, light curves. This is because we *naturally* 'see' or observe over long distances logarithmically. This has been shown experimentally, but is not taught in the mainstream. The linear method is adequate for global circumstances, but skews when we go galactic.

In my last book I revealed how I discovered Euler's number is built into the observer's equation when peering galactically. This is vitally important when calculating the age of the universe because it blows the Big Bang theory to smithereens! From your point of view, the only Big Bang that occurred was at your conception. To add credence to what I'm proposing, it has also been proven that indigenous people and young pre-educated children naturally count in a logarithmic fashion as opposed to linearly. The logarithmic/exponential function is built into the stock market and many other areas. It is literally everywhere.

In saying that, it's from this limited perspective that most of us function. For me, life was pretty straight forward until my forty first year and then my world turned upside down. You can either sink or swim. I chose to swim in the sea of hope. Many rational thinkers would see it as desperation, more like a sea of despair. As I keep repeating, life is all about perspective with no definitive right or wrong – it's always up to the individual. I've never given up hope of being with Robyn again; in fact I now know we will. Within the illusion of the stories the mind creates, the body will always perish. That is immutable, but remember you are not your body. You are much, much more!

ALIVE AND KICKING

The body is a human battery. Like all batteries, it runs out of electrical charge. Therefore the human body needs to be recharged (energised) on a regular basis. This is achieved via food, water and rest. On the face of it, food, water and rest do not appear to be related electrically, but they are.

Food at the fundamental level is composed of sunlight (information). Think about it. The food with the most nutritional content is grown outdoors or grazes outdoors eating grass etc. Fruits and vegetables either grow on trees or in the ground with their foliage utilising photosynthesis (sunlight) to grow. The wild and farm animals that we consume are much better for us than the battery chickens etc that are housed and processed in factories. The lack of natural sunlight and the poor grain they consume causes them to be nutritionally diminished, hence more sickness leading to the injection of anabolic synthetic hormones to counter. A diet heavily influenced by this process leads to a lack of energy and quite often sickness in the human body. Shite in equals shite out. The moral, make sure the majority of what you consume contains plenty of natural sunlight. Sunlight contains a spectrum of information, is the basic building block of food and along with water is the major requirement for life on earth.

John Ferris

> *"The light that resides in the sun shines light on all beings. It enters the earth as my being, for I nourish all things."*

> *The Bhagavad Gita*

What is the relationship between sunlight and electricity? The paradoxical dual nature of light is that it can travel both as a wave and at the same time as discreet particles known as photons. A photon is a single 'bit' of information with varying energy carried by electromagnetic radiation. Electromagnetic radiation is a force comprised of a spectrum of frequency wavelengths of electric currents and magnetic fields that run perpendicular to each other which together form the complex plane of the three dimensional reality you create and interact with. In other words everything you see, hear, touch, taste and smell is the electromagnetic force. You can take my word for it or go find out for yourself. I highly recommend the latter.

> *"If you want to understand the universe, think in terms of energy, frequency and vibration."*

> *Nikola Tesla*

It is only from biology's perspective that light acts as a wave or a photon (discrete particle). This is the dual nature of the mind. You can say a *wave* and a *particle* are opposites. One spread out everywhere, the other with a definite location in 'space and time' (duality). It is your mind which collapses the wave into a still frame 'picture with sound' (duality) of the world. In reality there is only one photon, one electron, one proton, one neutron, one anything! Fundamentally we can drop the proton and neutron (duality) – the nucleus of the atom as both are composed of quarks (interestingly the proton has two up and one down quark whilst the neutron has two down and one up quark. Can you see the fundamental pattern? (The power of three and the law of opposites). This is how the mind functions and when you understand this you get to pierce the veil of true reality – the nature of one whole infinite eternal absolute consciously aware entity. Look I'm only the messenger!

The other major requirement for life to thrive is water. Water hydrates the body and balances the impact of sunlight by preventing us from drying out. Everything in life is a balancing act! Our bodies are composed of roughly 70% water. The water in our bodies has many minerals which perform many bodily functions, but at a deeper level this mineralised water is a good conductor of electricity. Pure distilled water is not. Isn't it interesting that the earth's surface is also composed of approximately 70% water (connecting each of us fractally to Mother Earth) with the oceans made up of salt water which allows for the flow of electric currents and magnetic fields.

Last but not least is rest. A cessation of work or movement in order to relax, sleep or recover strength. There are stories of yogi's who go into deep meditation and do not move for six months or more, not eating or drinking in that time, but carry on living. Scientific studies have been conducted to show this to be the case. As discussed earlier, when at rest, what we have is a slow down in the electrical brainwave frequencies and when a state of dreamless sleep is entered your awareness is no longer in the world at large. You could argue you are now fundamentally plugged into the source of all – the power source!

IT'S TIME TO WAKE UP! IN MORE WAYS THAN ONE

Upon awakening, having recharged your body, it kicks into action. What is it then, that causes this action?

The smallest unit, of what we consider matter, is an atom. Everything is composed of atoms, including your body. If everything is composed of atoms, even the air you breathe, it stands to reason that you and the universe are in a constant state of flux. A constant energy exchange. Imagine being in a lift with a number of other people and somebody drops one. What you're breathing in is some of the atoms from... I'll leave it there. I'm sure you get the drift!!!

To be more precise; an atom is defined as the smallest constituent unit of ordinary matter that has the properties of a chemical element. The term 'chemical element' is key to our understanding. Quite often words have hidden meanings. By that I mean, when we read the words *chemical element* we tend to process superficially. We have a general sense of what it means when reading the sentence, but usually don't *fully* comprehend. We don't waste time in getting to grips with the nuts and bolts of what it is actually telling us.

Chemical relates to the interaction of substances, or something substantial, whilst element is something abstract. Abstract is something that exists as a thought, with no concrete existence – nothing substantial. Therefore the deeper meaning of the statement, an atom is the smallest constituent unit of ordinary matter that has the properties of a chemical element, is that this is the level or scalar dimension that the metaphysical becomes physical. This is where from your point of view as the observer, the *potential* for something to be, becomes an experience. It is the level of spiritual manifestation.

TAKE BACK CONTROL

Yet wrap your noggin around this. Nothing physical has taken place. It is only a mental perception of something physical. In a literal sense there never is anything physical... ever! There is no world 'out there' that actually exists physically. It does exist in a physical sense with sense being the operative word. The world 'out there' is a mental picture constructed via your brain and central nervous system (paradoxically including your brain and central nervous system) which only appears 'solid' due to the feedback of your sensory apparatus – sight, sound, taste, touch and smell interacting with the electromagnetic force expressed through you by source. When you tell people the world isn't solid they get their knickers in a twist exclaiming that it's a load of BS. Yet as always in duality there are two main reasons for why they find it hard to accept. The first is obviously because their own senses tell them different and secondly we are conditioned to believe what is socially accepted. Break out of the mould! Stop letting others pull your strings and take back control of your own story. It's you who is telling it anyway.

DAMN THAT BLOODY 'CHANGE'!

A month or so later, Karen and I ventured back into the coffee shop for a third time. To be fair I hadn't given my 'ufo' much thought in between, but that was about to change.

Once again Karen slipped off for her tanning session while I went in to place the order, but as I entered I was somewhat dismayed. The young waitress had changed from a mesmeric purple to a bleached blonde look, damn! The styling was still similar, but 'initially' to me less unique. As I looked for a seat I plucked up the courage to ask, "Are you the girl that had the purple hair?" knowing full well she was, followed by a gesticulated, "what have you done?" I continued, "The only reason I come here is to stare at your hair". Cheesy or what! I wouldn't go as far as to say she appeared flattered, but she did laugh and take it in good humour. I liked that. I liked the fact she could take it the way it was intended. That reflected back onto me. I felt good.

A few more pleasantries were exchanged before it was time to go. As I left, I was well aware that my 'ufo' was sitting at a table behind me facing in my direction. I wondered if I had made an impression. As I grabbed my stuff I glanced back and was pleased to see her looking up at me. She waved and shouted; "see you again!" with a beaming smile. I smiled back and gave her a thumbs up trying to look cool. In my mind I'd made an impression, in hers it was probably more like "£££! A potential new regular". I have no problem with that. I'm a business man myself. I know how it works! Pathetic really, but I walked out feeling half my age!

IT'S COMMON SENSE OR IS IT?

Some guy recently suggested to me to "Go play in traffic and get back to him". Charming... obviously I do understand his reasoning and am not offended.

On a side note, people play the victim card and get offended far too easily in today's society. This way of thinking is actually driven at the level of society by the mainstream narrative (political correctness gone rogue!) to keep people in a subservient victimised state of mind. When you recognise this and awaken to your true essence you realise it is you who is responsible for everything you experience within your own reality tunnel. When you assume responsibility, not only for your actions, but also what has appeared to happen to you, you can take control of the power within. This is when the magic happens!

I am not disputing that if a car hit me at high speed, in all likelihood, I would probably be seriously injured, at best. But materialists (those who believe a concrete world exists 'out there' whether an observer is present or not) are missing the point.

The *point* is your *point* of view. Everyone's spacetime reality tunnel is unique to them, I hope by now we all can agree on that. There are no two people who go through life having the same experiences at the same time and on top of that adding exactly the same meaning to those experiences.

Let's take a slight detour and go a little deeper. Bear with me. Einstein realised that two people moving relative to each other observing the same event always experience it a little differently. This might be microscopic, but never the less it's mind blowing.

Let's take the simple example of two observers. One observer is crossing the road whilst the other is driving a car. The driver loses control and the car strikes the pedestrian. Einstein realised no 'universal' story actually plays out. Here's why.

1) Neither observer can agree upon how much time passes between events.
2) They don't fully agree on how much space there is between things at any given moment.
3) They don't even agree on the chronological order of all the events.

Yet it has been proven that each observer measures things consistently and neither is wrong. Take this disagreement about sequence of events. If two observers can't agree on the sequence of events it means at present someone's past is in someone else's future. Therefore we can conclude there is no universal division of events into past, present and future. Once again here is proof eternity is real, with time being a unique construct of every biological being. You are fundamentally eternal, but from your biological *point* of view, you create your own unique spacetime reality tunnel which *is* time based. These are the staggering implications of special relativity. Each one of us is *special* relative to each other. Paradoxically this statement is saying we are all special. Once again do you see the pattern?

By establishing that no universal reality actually exists and that reality is created mentally by each observer, we confront possibly the ultimate paradox. What if two observers choose two opposing outcomes? The way the universe gets around this is not via parallel universes, as this would suggest space to be fundamental. No it's infinite versions of self which fits the bill much more eloquently.

Einstein's concept of special relativity demoted space and time as not fundamental. I don't think most people grasp what that implies. In layman's terms, it means the world you engage with everyday is not what you believe it to be. There is no solid, concrete world there, when you're not. This is nothing to be afraid of, quite the opposite, it empowers you. Einstein merged the two into a singularity and called it spacetime, which is now generally accepted as a way of explaining cause and effect (causality). The definition of spacetime is as follows: Spacetime (causality) refers to *whatever* external reality that underlies our *collective* experiences of the space between things and the time between events.

With Spacetime being defined as "*whatever* external reality" it must then be beyond mind and unable to be boxed, therefore infinite. The experimental evidence is giving us a glimpse of how infinity or 'all that is' expresses itself. Also we are told spacetime underlies our *collective* experiences of the space between things and the time between events. This must be due to each observer (conscious being) creating their own unique reality tunnel, with spacetime (infinite causality) somehow merging it all together.

On a side note, to incorporate gravity into his theory of special relativity, he postulated the concept of a spacetime fabric composed of light which gets warped when encountering objects with mass, which he called general relativity. This, when you think about it is just the observers perception of the angular momentum of perturbations of light which *we* perceive as objects. Gravity is the condensing of light spirals forming what you perceive as objects (objective reality) from *your* perspective. This is in effect electromagnetism in reverse; the feedback of information into the universe or 'all that is' at the level of the Planck scale, for those of a more scientific nature. Although general relativity lends itself well to understanding the universe at large mathematically, it has always been shown to be incomplete, which I am convinced is due to the misunderstanding of what gravity actually is.

Spiritual wisdom and the concept of the spacetime continuum are in total agreement; that everything is infinite and eternal which includes you and me (not as who you *think* you are but who you *really* are). Mainstream science is hindered by the system, as it's funded by the perceived 'powers that be' who do not want the populace becoming empowered and taking control of their own lives. In the event of this, the power exerted to control the masses fades into oblivion where it always was. It is only your belief or opinion that you need 'something' which gives it power. In reality you have no 'need' for anything. You might have a desire to 'experience' something which is your divine right, but that is different from needing it. Herein lies the paradox, due to the basic pattern of reality being a feedback loop, when you are experiencing your own personal story, the perceived 'powers that be' are always lurking in the shadows. The Swiss psychiatrist Carl Jung realised this and referred to it as *your* shadow psyche. You see, the 'powers that be' fundamentally are co-created by you due to the most basic feedback loop of all – the one and the many. With creation based on feedback embedded within itself then the primordial feedback loop must be oneness creating infinity creating oneness ad infinitum. An example of this being played out in recent years was the Occupy Wall Street movement which outed the so called 1%.

When you know the truth, you realise when you peer into the shadows there is only yourself looking back. This is you in an infinity of different guises, playing an infinite number of roles, all connected as one whole conscious awareness being aware of itself. We make the mistake of seeking the truth 'out there' in the imaginary story we have ourselves created in the belief that everyone else is experiencing the exact same story. We are all the one essence, imbued with the same power, experiencing differing versions of events of our own creation.

When telling *your* story, you encounter others who are telling theirs and when you take responsibility for your story you have dominion. When you accept and believe what others say 'at face value' you have given your power away.

"Think for yourselves and allow others the privilege to do so too"

Voltaire

What might be true for another might not be true for you and likewise what might work for you might not work for another. We have seen this play out many times in our lives, yet still tend to jump feet first onto the band wagon without due diligence.

With the understanding of infinite versions of self, you not only realise there are infinite versions of you but everyone else and everything else is you also. What we have is an infinity of infinities and herein lies the ultimate truth. As Voltaire says, tell your story and allow everyone else to tell theirs, even when you disagree as within the bigger picture it really doesn't matter.

VIBRATION IS THE KEY TO HAPPINESS!

All of the aforementioned means diddly squat unless I can provide a valid reason for how the world at large manifests in the way it does. The question still arises, "why in all likelihood will you feel pain if struck by an immaterial car of your own creation?" It is due to how your sensory apparatus functions and the beliefs you have chosen to accept throughout your lifetime.

Einstein's famous equation basically says that energy and mass are interchangeable. In other words they are the same thing. Everything in the universe is energy. Energy perpetually oscillates at different frequencies with information *informing* which frequency. This is the universal law of vibration. Therefore *energy* and *information* are also one and the same. Everything vibrates and is connected through vibration similar to tuning forks.

So how does the immaterial manifest as a solid, liquid or gas. The immaterial in this case is our thoughts and feelings. Thoughts can be measured electrically with every electric current producing a magnetic field. The opposite is true for a magnetic field, which is related to how we feel about something, producing an electric current. An electric current flows perpendicular to a magnetic field which produces a three dimensional complex holographic plane in which our spacetime reality plays out. This also includes the vessel we use to manoeuvre within this electromagnetic universe - our body. As Morpheus in the movie 'The Matrix' told Neo, your body is a residual self image, which is the mental projection of your digital self – an electromagnetic hologram.

Notice the pattern. As previously discussed, space and time were amalgamated to get a 'whatever' called spacetime (causality) which is based on cause and effect. Electricity and magnetism become electromagnetism which is the duality of light and sound propagating as an electromagnetic wave. Electromagnetic waves have energy and information which oscillate at a frequency that produces vibration. The vibrations interfere with each other creating interference patterns which when illuminated by light creates a hologram. Holograms are embedded fractally which are self similar repeating patterns at differing scales. This is the holofractographic nature of light interfering with itself at all scales.

For this process to mean anything a creative intelligent source must be present. This is where the duality of mind/body are fundamentally one at source. When two become one, we discover the fundamental principles of reality. Its all interconnected in a simple pattern based on an infinity of expressions connected by opposites.

A positive charge and an equal negative charge combine to cancel each other out to achieve neutrality, which is another way of saying nothing. So the immaterial is nothing until a *potential* difference, which is the definition of voltage/pressure (as both are the same thing), in charge occurs. This leads to an energetic electromagnetic manifestation taking place – a vibration. Ever wonder why the tingle feels so good!!!

BELIEVE IT OR BELIEVE IT NOT?

At a deeper scale, everything you perceive is immaterial. Your sensory apparatus is all based on vibration. Sight, hearing, taste, touch and smell all work in one way, by resonating at the same frequency of the vibrating atoms (charged particles) that you have not only created but are experiencing. Remember life is based on feedback. What's interesting is, you never actually touch anything. The positively charged atoms of your finger tips are repulsed by the positively charged atoms of the object, so in truth you really only ever come into contact with the space-in-between. It's this space-in-between that differentiates all objects (perturbations of light) in the material (enlightened) world. This is how everything is connected and made from the same thing, yet differentiates as all the variation we have come to enjoy in our quest for happiness. Fascinating or what?

Your personal beliefs are the other major player involved in how your life plays out. When you *awaken*, you realise life is a self fulfilling prophecy. What you believe to be true subconsciously (you could say the belief beneath your conscious thought) generally plays out. Does that make you right? Absolutely not. It is just your opinion, but the trick is, if you desire to have a particular experience, then believe it to be true and it will for you. This does not make it a fact for another.

"Everyone has a belief system (B.S.), the trick is to learn not to take anyone's B.S. too seriously especially your own"

Robert Anton Wilson

Some people believe in free will, others determinism. In actuality, you can make a case for both. Like everything it's a tangled hierarchy. If everything takes place in the one eternal moment of 'now' then of course it can be viewed as predetermined. But within *everything*, you as self awareness have the free will to choose whatever! What more could you want!

The higher spiritual self has total free will and dominion over everything in the one eternal moment with the *biological you* being the same, except for one major caveat - your belief system.

"Why do you stay in prison when the door is so wide open?"

Rumi

You are born as a child into the world as a free spirit with no conditions and no prejudices, but through your parents, peers, teachers and your own personal choices, over time you create mental barriers (sub-conscious programmes) with which you imprison yourself. What you believe to be true tends to be true, but only for you. Hence self fulfilling prophecies. Yet you will always witness others who can do more or perform better demonstrating your own personal restrictions that you have placed upon yourself.

Growing up and being constantly reminded to be careful when crossing the road, as it can be dangerous due to speeding cars, implants a belief that your life is endangered if you were to be struck by a car at speed. Now I can hear some of you saying, "Well John are you trying to tell us that if we tell our children that it is not dangerous to be struck by a speeding car because the bloody thing's immaterial they'll not get hurt! Really?" No I'm not saying that. Here's why. Even though you might continually reassure them that they cannot get hurt by a speeding car because the car is a construction of their own imagination, they most likely will come into contact with many other sources which will suggest different. On top of that you have the media which might portray a car accident or something similar which, of course, affects people's belief system immensely. It's a tricky game of probability, the essence of the quantum world, which your reality tunnel is built upon.

VIC'S WORDS OF WISDOM

The day after I left the coffee shop with a spring in my step, we met my best friend Keith and his wife Barbara in a trendy new restaurant in the big smoke. The big smoke in this case is Belfast, the capital of our wee country. It's a good half hour drive from San Fran Bangor where we live which in this country is an eternity for some. For most Bangorians, Belfast is a mythical place where they might venture once or twice a year. They are an indigenous people who don't really mix well. They tend to exhibit insular tendencies. Us - we're blow ins. We would venture to Belfast regularly. For those who have never been, it used to be a bit like the Gaza Strip, but in recent years it has risen from the ashes into a modern, vibrant city with lots to offer.

Having breakfast with Keith can be a challenging experience. In fact doing anything with Keith can be a challenging experience! "I only like to do what I want to do when I want to do it", he tells me on a regular basis. "Why would I want to go out with people I find boring, to places I find boring and be bored". As you can see he utilises the wholly trinity on a regular basis. If I told him this he would roll his eyes and shake his head in despair. I call him Vic when he's not about, as in Victor Meldrew. For those not in the know, Victor Meldrew is a much beloved British television character who is a grumpy aul git!

Having said all that, I have to say he makes me laugh. He is a very funny guy. Loads of one liners delivered like a true comedian; he's a true *barrel* of laughs! At times it strikes me that evolution has passed him by. Quite often he talks and thinks like people did in the 1970's. He keeps Barbara sweet by buying her the occasional frock. Who today calls a dress a frock!

As we sit having a late brunch, even later because the restaurant is short on kitchen staff, Karen spouts off about me the day before being all google eyed over the pretty waitress. Vic in typical Vic fashion reminds Karen she has absolutely nothing to worry about. "Listen Karen, as he sits there looking through his eyes seeing a gorgeous young girl, she's looking back through her eyes seeing an old pervert!!!

"I don't believe it!"

THE SMALLER YOU GO,
THE MORE YOU KNOW

Mention the term 'quantum physics' and everybody thinks you're an intellectual. Throw in quantum entanglement and everyone thinks you're a bore! "Didn't see him coming, will the next time!"

> *"If you think you understand quantum mechanics,*
> *you don't understand quantum mechanics"*
>
> *Richard Feynman*

> *"Everything we call real is made of things that cannot be*
> *regarded as real. If quantum mechanics has not profoundly*
> *shocked you, you haven't understood it yet."*
>
> *Niels Bohr*

Above are quotes from what's considered two of the greatest minds in physics. Niels Bohr and Richard Feynman as well as Einstein and many others appear to have fallen into the materialist trap. Physics is grounded in materialism: The theory or belief that *nothing exists* except matter and its movements and modifications; that matter is composed of particles and at the source of everything is a fundamental particle. When assumptions become so grounded, that even when all experimental evidence at the base level contradicts this and is continually ignored, you are on a hiding to *nothing*. Which ironically is exactly what they keep discovering – everything is made of *nothing*.

In an earlier chapter I discussed how all of mathematics is based on the empty set – *nothing*. At the base level of particle physics the assumption is that *virtual* particles of matter and anti-matter collide to create (bring into existence) little 'bits' of light (photons). Each tiny photon emits a little 'bit' of energy (light and sound) which can vary in luminosity and vibration, but all photons at this fundamental level exhibit the exact same amount of angular momentum (action). This field of photons is a quantum field of *action*, which you perceive as your reality tunnel – it's your imagination (image-in-*action*).

If we ask where do these *virtual* particles of matter come from? We are told that they come from *nothing*! With the confirmation that light has no mass and travels nowhere, it is only when *you* the observer act as a reference point that light appears to travel at a set speed, surely must put the *biological* you front and centre!

As I've previously mentioned, in particle physics, the most fundamental particles discovered thus far, which make up protons and neutrons, are called quarks. Interestingly both the proton and the neutron have three quarks each (wholly trinity) and are the opposite to each other. When you ask a quantum physicist what quarks are composed of, they will tell you that they are waves of probabilities. A probability wave is *nothing* tangible. All roads home lead to nothing.

*Above captured on camera for the first time ever,
is a glimpse of what reality truly is!*

The fact that everything is *nothing* is nothing to be alarmed about. You and everything else have always been nothing. Eastern wisdom has been informing us of this for aeons. It is you who makes nothing become something. This is what is known as subject – object expression; with you always acting as the subjective observer creating and deciding what your objective creation means. This is quantum entanglement which in classical real world terms is *your* relationship to everything else. It is your focused attention of mind. Where attention goes, energy flows. Knowing this leads us to the conclusion that the purpose of life is experiencing 'whatever' you decide and 'whatever' you decide it to be.

"Quantum physics tells us that nothing that is observed is unaffected by the observer. That statement, from science, holds an enormous and powerful insight. It means that everyone sees a different truth, because everyone is creating what they see."

Neale Donald Walsh

What is really fascinating is that quantum physics is considered the most accurate science of them all. The greatest scientific minds might see it as gobbledy gook, but still realise this really is how the world works. To them it might as well be a giant multicoloured spaghetti monster because their rational thought processes get turned upside down entangled inside out!

"Shut up and calculate"

Richard Feynman

This was the famous quote by Feynman to his students when they attempted to comprehend philosophically the meaning of the quantum world. Just do the maths and the answers will take care of themselves and don't worry about the how and why.

Quite simply, the quantum world is the opposite to the world we live in. In the quantum realm, location and time do not exist. Everything is spread out as a wave of potential or probability wave until an observer 'collapses the wave function' into a discreet 'still' reference frame. This is the power of choice (consciousness) at work with consciousness moving from one still frame to the next, composing a unique story as it does so, through each one of us.

In the outer world, everything is perceived by mind to have a 'location in space at any given moment in time'. The key word here is moment. We live in duality with moment referring to both angular momentum (everything spins) and also 'now' (timeless). What we have is a 'still' reference frame of potential movement. Just like a 'frame' in a movie reel that when put through a projector plays out as one still frame after another to create the experience of movement. Hence the movie projector, from your perspective, is your brain playing a mental projection. After reading this if you feel like your head's in a spin, it quite literally is!

Look, the above is a simple fundamental explanation of quantum theory. Like anything in our world we love to extrapolate and become entangled in our own web of creation. Why see the simplicity in reality, when you can go off down the rabbit hole and concoct a cacophony of stories that will lead to confusion, providing you with more questions than answers to satisfy your thirst to continually discover more scientific clap trap! When related to the theory of everything (TOE), western science has become a religion to the great deity of logic and robotic observation and measurement.

I'm no "quantum physicist". I don't need to be. I've never been taught about it in a classroom or university. I'm self schooled and due to the way today's society is totally pigeon holed, this makes it the only way to see the bigger picture. When I wrote my last book I had not set out to discover the pattern to reality, but as I put pen to paper with all the jumbled thoughts in my head out it popped, singing and dancing. You could say the pattern of reality, life's dance, discovered me.

By applying this fundamental pattern - a feedback loop based on opposites with you as the interface and the realisation that opposites are paradoxically one and the same - the answers will fall into place. *From our perspective*, the *quantum world will never be fully understood by mind because it is mind*. What we can do is become aware of the process and pattern by which it functions. It's your mental perspective which is the subject entangled with the object of the focus of your attention combined with intention.

A MIND DERANGED? OR
JUST REARRANGED!

My desire in life is a big one, no half measures here. It is to be reunited with my daughter Robyn. It is to reset the clock and this time keep my family together and healthy. I guess when they say you should aim for the stars I've taken it literally. I know the thought on most people's minds is, has he lost the plot! I totally understand this but there are those of us who know differently. Everything I have come to know and understand has all been fuelled by this one question - can you change the past?

I am well aware the general consensus is No! But if we never pushed the general consensus boundaries we would never have taken to the skies, sailed the oceans, climbed the highest mountains, peered into the quantum world and observed the farthest galaxies. Have you ever asked yourself how does a telephone work? Where does a text message go when it gets lost in cyberspace? And where the heck *is* cyberspace?

All of the above originated in someone's imagination and by going deeper you then realise that everyone's imagination is your imagination. Bet you didn't realise you were that smart. Well you are! You have just got to learn to open up your mind. It takes character to address not only the tough situations and circumstances that life throws at you, but also character to overcome these challenges.

THE BIGGEST CHARACTERS MAKE THE BIGGEST IMPACT

One facet of life is about meeting characters and my mate Keith (Vic) certainly fills that mould. Characters come in all shapes and guises. Being a personal fitness trainer, working with many people from all walks of life, I have come across a few over the years. Their personalities tend to dominate somewhat, for better or worse, but always leave a lasting impression.

My colleague Michael, who works from my studio, is one. The events of his life are like an entire series about Frank Spencer. You couldn't write the script, honestly! Another would be Jim, who fathered 'the actual' Mr. Grey! Actually, when I think about it, Jim has never stopped fathering - he's an obstetrician. Jim is a thinker, he never stops! He once asked me, "What exactly is meditation?", "simple meditation is about focusing on your breath and allowing your thoughts to fade away to the point of no thought", was my response. "Sod that" was Jim's.

He's getting on a bit, yet having semi-retired from the doctor hood, has no idea how to slow down. Perpetually active, he travels the world on top of coming up with new innovative business ideas. This time next year he'll be a millionaire! One such idea was playing football in a circle with the net at the centre. Novel I thought, nice idea but... then he suggested I go away and develop it further. I came back with the name 'Circular Soccer' and before I knew it, he had 'me' running around in circles. That's Jim. An ideas man and brilliant networker. He discovers the well and the rest of us do the drilling.

These are the people that you draw into your life to spice things up, make you laugh and sometimes end up leaving you devastated. My daughter Robyn was one for sure, even at her tender years she was larger than life itself.

Another was Robbie Millar. Robbie was a client of mine for seven years and became a good friend. He had a scintillating personality, loud, brash and was very tactile often greeting you with a bear hug or a punch on the arm. Anybody that knew Robbie would attest to this. He was a Michelin star chef of ten years who many considered the best in the country. In the early hours of a rain soaked morning he lost control of his car and was killed instantly. I received the news the next day upon entering work and to say I was devastated is an understatement. People die, its part of life. Some are expected, others not. But there are some who you just can't imagine ever dying, at least not until they're old. These are the people who jump on the saddle and take the reigns of life by the horns and ride it like a John Wayne or girls, a Calamity Jane!

John Ferris

Robbie's accident affected me deeply. It surprised my mum how deeply. I don't remember crying much as a kid and through to my forty first birthday. On that day everything changed.

GIVE ME A CHILD UNTIL HE IS 7 AND I WILL SHOW YOU THE MAN

I come from a small family. I was born on the epiphany, January 6th 1967. At that moment and for the foreseeable future, my immediate family consisted of three people; my mum, my nana and my uncle John who I was obviously named after. I never met my father. My mum left him and travelled back home to Belfast from South End on Sea where she had been married and lived for two years. She only found out she was pregnant days after returning home. She sent a letter to his father, but never received a reply, so I'm told. Who knows if he received it? Either way it led to 'wee Johnny' being brought up by his mum and nana. Years later my mum confessed that they did worry a little, that with no father figure, I might grow up to be 'wee Nancy'. I can assure you there was no need to worry on that front. Ironically, Robyn's middle name is Nancy, after Karen's mum. This somehow happened after Karen apparently was so opposed to middle names that when Jordan, our eldest was born, she talked me out of giving him the middle name Wilson, which is mine. I guess this still rankles. No doubt when I grow up I'll get over it.

Years later my mum married Alfie, my stepfather and shortly after, along came my little sister. There is almost ten years between Paula and me, although now you wouldn't think it! Apart from my nana, Jordan and Robyn, this leaves my uncle John (we all have one... or Bob in some cases), his kids; Geordie and Ryan and my nieces; Holly and Faye as the only blood relatives I have met in my lifetime. In saying that, you do feel like you knew the others through the stories handed down and feel an affinity towards them.

Looking back, growing up on a West Belfast estate at the top of the notorious Shankill road provided me with an interesting grounding. Although I had numerous friends in and around the street where we lived and with plenty happening, I still felt isolated and lonely at times, having to wile away many an hour by myself. Especially when it rained. As a child I wasn't allowed out in the rain and boy did it rain plenty. Years later after moving to Glengormley, Keith's mother would label me as delicate because of this. We still laugh about this today. Nobody else has ever thought of me as delicate. Growing up in Highfield ingrained a tough streak that has at times stood me in good stead and at others most certainly not!

My nana was born in Belfast, but emigrated with her mother and younger brother to Philadelphia at the age of five. She spent eighteen years in the States before having to return to sunny Northern Ireland during the depression, due to her mother, Maggie Smith having never taken out American citizenship.

It probably would have served Maggie better to have stayed because years later during a typical Norn Iron downpour she was unfortunately knocked down and killed by a black taxi on the Ballygomartin road.

My nana was a very loving and well presented woman, but could be very tough and stubborn, probably due to having to provide for my mum and uncle throughout the Second World War whilst my grandfather swanned off fighting at Dunkirk and the like. George Wilson was a tough Sergeant Major in the British army, who as I've mentioned, fought at Dunkirk ending up lying in a ditch for forty eight hours with a severe chest wound. He would survive this, serving his country for many more years, but eventually succumbing to emphysema, brought on by the Dunkirk episode, on New Year's Eve of 1952. Unfortunately for him, he was a Mancunian, born just thirty five miles from Gods promised land, that of Liverpool. Now that's a football club! His saving grace in my eyes was that he supported City over United.

This strength of character, from both parents, rubbed off on my mum and uncle. When the war ended, after a stint in Hamburg, the family moved into 8 Highvale Gardens, the same street I later grew up in, on the Highfield estate. I remember being told how eight weeks after my uncle had broken his arm; he and my Nana had to walk to the hospital and back to get his plaster removed. It was a six mile round trip. Later that evening he broke the other arm which he kept secret until he rolled over on it in bed and they had to repeat the trip. From what I heard, after my nana got hold of him, the newly broken arm was the least painful part of his body.

Another was when my nana and grandfather had gone out for the evening and for the first time, my uncle, being four years older than my mum was left in charge. After stoking the coal fire, he left the red hot poker lying on the hearth which my mum, barefooted, proceeded to stand on. Her foot was really badly burnt, but he convinced her to not tell on him as they would not allow him to look after her again. She went to bed in severe pain only to waken in the middle of the night crying in agony. Another midnight trip to the hospital ensued. My nana suggested to the hospital, another bed might be required for my uncle too.

In 1959 my nana got her long awaited wish and immigrated back to Philadelphia along with mum. My uncle was to stay at home for a further six months to complete his five year engineering apprenticeship in James Mackies. Three months after my nana upped sticks and replanted roots in where she always considered home, in walked Johnny boy. No patience, no apprenticeship. Only for the fact he was now fully grown he would probably have gotten another pasting!

My uncle developing itchy feet beside my mum and nana as they're about to emigrate to America.

Unfortunately for my nana, a year later my mum and her set sail on the Queen Mary crossing the Atlantic, to return to her real home for good. My mum was 16 at the time and just couldn't settle in the states. There is something magical about Northern Ireland. Even with all its infighting and hatred there is still a strong sense of community and friendship. As we already know in the world 'out there' - opposites attract.

My uncle stayed, serving two years in Korea having been drafted into the American army. Soon after, he met Kathy, a Philly native who he would marry, have two boys with and spend the rest of his days. You think my family are characters; you want to meet my Aunt Kathy's. Mine pales into insignificance compared to hers!!!

The war and its trials were ingrained in people's memories and provided deep rooted conditioning. For all its negatives it was immensely character building, not only for those who fought, but also those who had to endure it. This conditioning gets passed down through the generations, not only through the regaling of stories, but also the media especially Hollywood movies and the like, eventually fading over time. The war not only had a profound effect on my family, as I'm sure it did with most families of that era, but also on me. I would hear a number of stories about my grandfather, my great grandfather on my nana's side who died in the trenches in France in 1915 and other family members who fought and died for their country. Stories help to condition minds. The stories I would hear as a young child not only instilled a strong mentality in me, but also a deep sense of love and empathy. In life opposites play the most vital role. From adversity springs joy! This is why I'll never give up hope in my quest to be reunited with my daughter Robyn. I know in my heart and also after much research, but more importantly intuitive soul searching, that everything is possible!

A WORLD SHATTERED

It was early December 2007. My mum was taken into hospital again. This scenario had been playing out more frequently in recent years especially when portable oxygen was provided to help her breathe. When she was ten years old she had developed pneumonia and was left with a scar on her lung. Over the years she had been susceptible to chest infections and as time passed her aerobic capacity had diminished considerably. I didn't realise then, but greater potency leads to less time. Heisenberg's uncertainty principle playing out classically. The more energy something contains the quicker it burns out with the opposite also true. This is why the air we breathe is only 21% oxygen and not the mega dose my mum was ingesting. Too much of anything is not a good thing. In my mums case I guess it was a balancing act between the quality or quantity of life. Two years with mobility, although restricted somewhat by the oxygen tank, or possibly three or four housebound without. I'm not sure though if she was afforded the choice by the doctors.

Unfortunately this time my mum would not survive this hospital visit. It was an incredible shock to me as over time you just become accustomed to the pattern that when she went into hospital she would come back out. I was devastated.

My mum was 64 years old, comparatively young in today's standards. Little did I know what was just around the corner.

Like most of us, I loved my mum very much. As I pointed out earlier nothing stands still, everything changes and as you go through life and especially when you have your own family, priorities change. Just days before my mum passed I remember she made an unusual comment. It referred to both Jordan and Robyn and if how anything ever happened to them... I thought it was a bit left field at the time. Only Robyn was in the vicinity and it was Robyn she looked at. Robyn upon hearing her looked up at me and to this day her facial expression is imprinted in my mind.

I am now aware that in every given situation we read 'whatever' we choose to into it; not only in the moment, but also create stories about it retrospectively. Knowing this, does that make it less real? I would say no, not at all. This is reality, this is how it works and paradoxically there is nothing more real.

At this stage in my life, the story I started unwittingly to tell myself turned into my worst nightmare. It not only brought me to my knees, but the rest of my family too. Just prior to Christmas and a few weeks after my mum's passing my six year old daughter Robyn began to get headaches. At the time, Karen and I didn't realise that it is rare for young children to get headaches, never mind almost daily. Robyn's eyes were very heavy with her reflexes somewhat diminished. Looking back I cannot believe how oblivious we were to Robyn's symptoms at the time.

On Boxing Day Karen took Robyn to accident and emergency to get checked out. It was then that I first began to feel a little worried. The doctor sent her home saying she might have picked up some sort of virus and joked at least it's not a brain tumour! It was something I had not even considered and I remember thinking what the hell!

About ten days later, it was the day before my forty first birthday, the four of us went to a nice restaurant for a family meal to celebrate. In the interim period Robyn's headaches had been sporadic, but as we sat down to eat it was obvious Robyn was in a lot of discomfort. Midway through the meal we got up and left going straight to the hospital.

We arrived at the hospital for Robyn to be admitted for overnight observation. Karen stayed with her while I took Jordan home. Early the next morning, Jordan and I went back to the hospital with the drive up being particularly tormenting. My sister Paula and her family called up to the hospital to see Robyn and to give me my birthday present, at which time Robyn and Jordan did so too. I couldn't think of a worse place to be. All hope faded of Robyn being discharged when a couple of hours later the results of the cat scan came through. We were informed there was an issue, but more investigation was necessary.

The following day Robyn bravely underwent an MRI. Karen was allowed in and held her hand throughout. Robyn took it in her stride. Me... not so. I was pacing for an hour in the waiting area and knew from the body language of the radiologist that things were not good. That afternoon, Karen and I were brought into a small room to be told our beautiful daughter was diagnosed with a brainstem glioma and that there was nothing the doctors could do. To say we were floored is the biggest understatement imaginable! The emotional pain we felt was so intense that words fail. How could our little girl who was rarely sick, become so ill? On average, only two children per year in Northern Ireland are diagnosed with such a condition.

A day later upon meeting the oncologist we were told Robyn would probably have between six to twelve months. I remember feeling a twisted sense of relief that we would have at least some time with her, but also knowing it is not enough and acceptance is not on the table. We were told that radiotherapy would be required to achieve this timeline and chemotherapy was an option, but unlikely to make much difference. We said we would do anything, if there was even a one percent chance that Robyn could survive.

What we did not realise was the word 'terminal' is just a western medical term used in cases when western medical practices statistically have no long term impact. Treating with radiation and chemotherapy are their methods of choice. Both are extremely toxic to the human body. Both have the potential to poison surrounding healthy cells as well as depleting the only thing that ever heals – your own immune system. All drugs mask symptoms. There has never been a drug in the history of drugs that has ever healed anyone. It is your own immune system which is the healer. Think of it this way. Say you have a deep infected cut. You can treat it with antiseptic creams and bound the wound to prevent an infection, but ultimately it is your immune system which performs the healing. This is the same for cancer. Yes there are many cases where tumours are shrunk by radiation and/or chemotherapy drugs and in some cases the cancer is completely eradicated, but they are much fewer than you think. Many cancers do return having spread throughout the body, potentially due to a weakened immune system. I am not saying do not follow medical advice (ironically it's forbidden anyway), I'm just saying there are many other options available if you choose to go a different root.

Neither Karen or I had ever experienced any close friends or loved ones contract 'terminal' cancer so at the time we felt completely at the mercy of the so called 'professionals'. Over the next seven months, being at the coal face of the cancer industry, we discovered so much and I can tell you without any shadow of a doubt it *is* an industry – a money making industry of the highest immoral order!

Don't get me wrong, the doctors, nurses and support staff who work in this environment on a daily basis do so with the best intentions. It is just unfortunate that the main players have been unwittingly brainwashed by the pharmaceutical industry to accept their for profit policies over the highest welfare of the individual human being.

A CORPORATE VIRUS

The cancer industry is sick. In the 1950's one in ten were likely to get cancer in their lifetimes. Around the millennium it was one in three. As of late, we are being told it's one in two. Billions of dollars are being poured into the treatment and search for a cure every year. A high proportion of that money comes from charities that tap into your empathetic self to extract another stealth tax from your hard earned wages. This money drives the search for more very expensive synthetic chemotherapy drugs which quite often attempt to mimic natural remedies available in nature. We have also been brainwashed into believing natural remedies aren't as potent or as effective as chemotherapy drugs. Absolute bullshit! We are told every drug must go through a seven year clinical trial to make sure of its safety and that natural remedies aren't safe because this procedure is not enforced. It is not enforced because the law states anything that is natural cannot be patented and sold for extortionate profit. Every cancer patient is a customer of the pharmaceutical behemoth. It would scare you how profitable you are when you are being treated for cancer.

The pharmaceutical industry owns and subsidises the medical schools which then support their money making agenda. They only accept 'grade A' students because the educational system has been so dumbed down that the pupils with the best ability to regurgitate information now come out on top. This leaves the creative thinkers (who question the system) getting lost in the mire. Guess who are the easiest people to brainwash? The information processors! Just like Feynman said "shut up and calculate". Of course I'm not saying *every* 'grade A' student is not a creative thinker. Back in the 1900's, the biggest industries in the world were oil and steel. Now it's the tech giants and pharmaceuticals.

When Robyn was first diagnosed I had asked what foods should she consume more of and what should she avoid. The oncologist looked at me blankly and said he didn't know; that it was not something they considered for treatment. I later found out that most doctors spend about one week on nutrition over the course of 7 years of training. Maybe I'm missing something, but would you not think it would be better to keep people healthy as opposed to managing illness? If I may, healthy people aren't profitable from a western medical point of view.

I graduated as a mechanical engineer. I later moved into the fitness industry where I have over 20 years experience. I have worked with hundreds of clients in that time and one thing I can say for sure – if you eat healthily, live in a healthy environment and have a positive outlook in life, your risk of cancer or any serious illness diminishes in accordance. It doesn't mean you won't get sick, but the probability lessens dramatically. The question we then must ask, "Are doctors trained as health practitioners or disease and illness managers?" Remember the old adage 'a pill for every ill'. We can extrapolate that to "a pill for every ill puts money in the pharmaceutical till – Ker-Ching! Bastards!"

As of writing in 2017 and after all the major technological advances and billions, if not trillions, poured into the pharmaceutical industry over the years, the stats show you are five times more likely to get cancer than you were only sixty years ago. The cancer industry *is* sick!!! Rant over.

MUM'S THE WORD

A few days pass and after Vic's wise words, I find myself drawn towards the coffee shop. I feel more energised than I have in a while. This time though, I'm on my own – I managed to ditch the bitch! Yee hah! Years of being stuck to me like a leech. At last, freedom from the Mrs! Hahaha! Of course, I'm only joking! I think it's more like Karen's been itching for years to get rid of me!

Seriously though, I don't have any ulterior motive, but there is an attraction. I can guess what most of you are thinking, is he soft in the head? - the attraction is blatantly obvious. Believe it or not, this is different. At this juncture I struggle to understand why myself. I have witnessed many a pretty waitress in a multitude of coffee shops, but don't feel drawn to the coffee shop because of them. Why is this different? They say timing is everything. We are all drawn to inspirational, energetic experiences that people and places provide. That hit of dopamine that doesn't require a bong or rolled up dollar bill. Sometimes it's just engaging with someone who is willing to give you their time and attention that appeals to you. It helps when you feel comfortable and relaxed in the surroundings. I've come to realise that giving someone your attention for a period of time is much more beneficial and uplifting than giving them money or material things.

Feeling 'jaded' with life, turning fifty, every so often noticing an overnight facial earthquake having taken place forming a new canyon, but still feeling very much like you're twenty five, you do wonder what the world looking back sees and thinks. I do know it doesn't matter what anyone else thinks, it only matters what you think, as you are the creator, but years of being conditioned in the opposite fashion still makes you question in moments of weakness. The vanity of life – me?.....never! Okay well maybe now and again.

It's relatively quiet inside with only two other customers sitting further down and one other staff member who spends most of her time talking with them. It's not long before I strike up a conversation with my ufo. With the shop being quiet, she seems happy to stand and talk. She laughs and smiles a lot as we converse about the local coffee shop culture, amongst other things. There's no doubt I did flirt a little. It's one of the few pleasures a man of my years can still have. All above board, nothing outrageous, to me just a bit of fun. She played along being very polite. I mentioned Vic's old pervert quote, she laughed and said "No not at all", twice, the second probably trying to convince herself! I laughed. All in all I found her very engaging, interesting and up lifting. You know what, we all live in a bubble of our own construction and for the most part, we engage with people of a similar generation but when you step outside and fill your lungs with the freshness of change, you feel liberated. I was well aware that it was me driving the conversation throughout. She was more than happy to get involved in the topics, but didn't ask me much. Not that I have much of a problem with that, as when I get going I can talk! Some of my clients who come to exercise not only get a physical workout, but a mental one too.

When it was time to pay, the young girl was in the kitchen, so the other member of staff did the till. At that moment, one of the customers who had been sitting further down the shop turned to me and asked, "Does Michael work in your studio?" My first thought was, what seriously? "Yes, actually he does, how did you know?" I said. "I overheard you mention you had a personal training studio in Holywood, he's my cousin". I laughed and thought you can get away with nothing in this country. At times I can be too loud for my own good... not that I was up to no good! I then spent another 10 mins or so regaling a number of Frank Spencer moments in the life and times of our Michael. She had a few of her own! To top it all off, it turns out that the other staff member privy to my conversation was the owner who happens to be my ufo's mum!!!

Anyhow, as I was leaving my ufo was bringing in the chairs and tables from outside as it was closing time. Doesn't time fly when you're having fun! I approached her saying "my names John, by the way, actually just John, and you are?" with the most beautiful smile she replied "Jade".

Jade

IT'S SMILES BETTER

Robyn also has a smile that would light up any room. It's a gift. The people who walk among us that can greet another with the broadest, warmest and most open of facial expressions have a profound effect on the rest of us. It makes people feel better about themselves and when you can have that effect on others it is something very special. I remember many times telling Robyn that she talks with her eyes. When she was passionately telling me something she would draw me into those beautiful greyish blue eyes where I would feel totally immersed in love, quite often losing the thread to what she was saying, followed by a "daddy!" I am so glad I imprinted those moments onto my heart because I can bring them back at any time and relive as if they were happening right now. Do you know what? The reason I can do that and you too is because what you vividly imagine is as real, in the one eternal moment, as what you believe your moment to moment reality to be.

We are time travellers - all of us. You have complete authority and dominion over time. You are a time lord. You time travel all of the *time*! Generally not realising it. When you fell from grace, a metaphorical description of your spiritual self being born into the world, you were without prejudice or mental restrictions. You were innocent, non local, timeless awareness, born into an illusory spacial dimension (personal reality tunnel) creating your own experience of time for the purpose of telling your own unique story. *Yes* we are all gods! The absolute self (godhead) in a sense is schizophrenic. God or pure conscious awareness is the totality of every individual self with every individual self also being an aspect of many selves. Here we have an infinity of infinities – the opposite to nothing. We think we are a singular aspect, but in reality each of us is a schizophrenic version of God, the infinite or singular self. It's all perspective folks! The secret to comprehending this and fundamental reality is getting to grips with how the feedback loop of the one and the many or nothing and infinity is all the same thing. How one entity is simultaneously individuated into many aspects of itself, with each aspect having the power of the whole from a different perspective without realising.

You are not the same person you were ten years ago. You are not even the same person you were five years ago, in fact at a minuscule level you are not the same as a moment ago. We all exhibit habitual traits which disguise this fact, with some being carried throughout our lifetime, but we all evolve... admittedly at different rates!

Looking back over my fifty years, I am not the young boy having just watched John Wayne playing Davy Crocket, standing on my stairs at home battling the hoards of Mexican soldiers about to invade my imaginary Alamo. I am no longer the teenager with a crush on Heather, the beautiful girl a year below me, who dreamed one day of holding her in my arms and being swallowed up into her beautiful grey eyed gaze. Neither am I the uninspired aerospace engineer, who dreaded spending eight hours colouring in charts and producing graphs for accountants to cost. I am no longer the footballing genius who scored goals for fun on a Sunday morning, dribbling by people as if they were standing still... *well* that's how I remember it! With regret, I am no longer experiencing Jordan and Robyn as young children when they were growing up, which I cherished *so* much. Now that I have turned fifty I am none of those Johns and yet I am *all* of them. I am forever travelling in non-linear time, spiralling back and forth, forever experiencing *the* one eternal moment in an infinity of ways.

This though is only a small sample of who I am. I am everything I have ever watched on television and read in a book. I am every tree, car and insect I have ever imagined into being and come into contact with. I am even every person I have ever met or heard about. Yes, I am you and you are me. We are just different versions of the same self. We are infinite and eternal. When you grasp the enormity of who you are and the power you possess deep within, you realise time is a notion you embrace at the biological level simply for the purpose of telling yourself a story. Unfortunately like me we quite often fuck it up!... but all is not lost. Nothing is ever lost. It is the potential to be '*al*ways' in 'all ways'.

CHEERS EVERYONE

As the months have passed I have now made it to regular status in Jade's eyes. She has now started to take the piss! I venture into the coffee shop two to three times per week now. I feel like Norm from cheers. I have my go-to seat, which I advocated they keep free for me and I proposed that when I arrive I say "hey everyone" and the guys all shout back in unison "John!" Well at least these were my suggestions until I discovered none of them had ever watched the t.v. Show Cheers, never mind heard of Norm. Sometimes it can prove challenging to be witty with the younger generation. Now that I think of it, I remember when I was young thinking how unfunny a lot of older people were. Ho hum, I suspect it's that fifty year noose hanging around my neck at play again.

I think I might have taken it a bit far

BACK TO THE FUTURE

Have you heard of the grandfather paradox? This is what mainstream science uses to debunk time travel. It's very simple. One day you wake up and decide you want to travel back in time, so you build yourself a time machine. Just like that. If you just heard Tommy Cooper's voice in your head I can safely say, you're of an age! You travel back in time to when your grandfather was alive and before you were born. Due to an extremely careless error in judgement you kill him. The question is "how could you have travelled back if you were never born in the first place?" Herein lies the grandfather paradox.

For the mainstream this paradox appears to put the nail in your grandfather's coffin, ending any potential for time travel. Having gotten this far *can* you see the blatant misconception? The mainstream makes the mistake of continually objectifying time. Time is *not* an object, it is subjective. Therefore it is pointless trying to build a time travel machine, which of course is an object. As I've said you are already time-travelling regularly in your *imagination.*

I wanna tell you a story. If you've just heard Max Bygrave's voice in your head that's clarification! Anyway, sit back, take a moment and relax. Ok, what I want you to do is imagine a lemon in your minds eye. A zesty, juicy lemon. Also imagine a serrated knife. Now imagine using the knife to cut the lemon into quarters. Imagine lifting one of the juicy quadrants and biting into it. Have you just had a saliva response? I should think so. If not a visit to your doctor is in order.

What has just happened is your *immaterial* imagination has elicited a perceived *material* experience which you created. Now answer this. Where was the lemon before I asked you to think of it? If you're unsure - the answer is... both *nowhere and now-here*. It didn't exist yet it paradoxically always exists. From your biological (human) perspective the lemon didn't exist until you created it and brought it into your personal reality tunnel. From your true self's perspective, everything exists always and in all ways. Are you beginning to see the pattern? Due to opposite perspectives both being equally correct a paradox always arises. This paradox from your biological perspective is impossible to comprehend because mind defines everything via paradoxical feedback loops. Yet you are *aware* that the paradox exists. This is key to understanding at source you are not your mind. Your mind is an emergent property of pure, timeless awareness and it's this awareness that you truly are – whatever that is.

"You are not a drop in the ocean. You are the entire ocean in a drop"

Rumi

To summarise, through your imagination you conjured a thought in your mind to bring the lemon into your reality tunnel (which you perceive as existence) and created an experience which through a mental feedback loop you informed awareness of what it meant to you – your opinion. Everything you perceive in your reality tunnel works in the same way only you might utilise more of your *imagined* sensory apparatus to create a more *tangible* experience. Perception is imagination and you are the imagination of yourself. This *is* reality creation. Reality tunnels are models of reality, *not* reality itself, a common misconception. *This is the way, the truth and the life* of the story you tell yourself.

"Imagination is more important than knowledge"

Einstein

By using his imagination Einstein merged space and time into the singularity of spacetime. What he really discovered through his imagination was the collective of everyone's imagination – the amalgamation of causality. Due to infinity being unmeasurable, the more important question science cannot address is; who or what is the observer or awareness behind imagination?

LIFE'S ABOUT LIVING AND ACCEPTING

When telling the story of your life (imagining) on a moment to moment basis, inspiration plays a vital role. Inspiration is inspired-action, which just like everything else, is cloaked in mystery. What inspires one person might be the epitome of complete boredom for another. Music can be inspirational. It can empower you and make you feel like a God or it can scare the bejesus out of you. Try watching a horror movie with the volume turned down. You will discover that the fear factor has completely disappeared. Turn the volume up and suddenly you are emotionally involved once more. Awesome! I love to listen to inspiring music when I read a book. Try it as you read these pages and see if it lifts you. There are many ways we inspire ourselves, remember it's only you who's choosing how to perceive your story. Me? I seem to get inspired by girls with short purple hair! It could be worse. I remember reading in the newspaper many years ago about a guy who was continually arrested for being inspired to stick his winkle in the cracks of pavements. No shit!

Admittedly there might be a little more to it than just Jade's hair; they do sell delicious food and good coffee! Circumstances and timing always play a vital role. I guess Jade was just unfortunate to be in the wrong place at the wrong time hahaha! Life's a bitch and then you marry one. Shit, better not go there or she'll bar me. It wouldn't be the first time she has threatened to, yes mum... that sense of humour of mine again!

Look, to be honest, I'm really only amusing myself. I was feeling bored with life so concocted a narrative to lift my spirits. We all do it at different times in different ways. As long as people are not impacted in a negative way then what's the harm? There is no serious intent on my part to impact on Jade's life. She has her family and I have mine. What she has done, in a completely unintentional way, is to help lift me out of my ageing doldrums and inspire me into a new lease of life. I look at it as therapy... talk therapy. By forming new relationships, allowing you the opportunity to spout your personal story whilst engaging in theirs, opens up an avenue for stagnated energy to circulate. It's certainly much cheaper than the American way of paying a small fortune to a shrink!

You could say Jade is my muse (a person or personified force who is the source of inspiration for a creative artist). Karen reckons instead of the word creative I should insert piss!... Charming! Moving swiftly on, Jade has enlightened me on a number of occasions that I tend to over think things. After much consideration I think she's right! Life is not all about thinking, it's also about observing without judgement and accepting, which allows the more powerful inner self to flow and bring about your heartfelt desires. I know I must accept that Robyn has gone and be able to let go, otherwise how can I ever get her back. Acceptance can be so difficult.

IT'S SOMETIMES BETTER TO CRACK AN EGG THAN TO CRACK A JOKE!

I must admit that I did feel, on the odd occasion, a little weird when I went in for coffee. I maybe over egged it at times attempting to be funny or interesting. (Vic recently informed me what I think is funny nobody else does! Not one for mincing his words is our Vic! Speaking of mincing, he has a strong resemblance to Julian Simmons). Maybe its why early on I found Jade a challenge to engage with at times. I would crack a joke; she would crack a smile while thinking plonker! I suspect she didn't fully get my sense of humour, that bloody generational gap again and possibly didn't understand my motives even though I did address that my intentions were honourable. I guess it's understandable. Some character shows up out of the blue and announces he's writing a book which you are very much a part of. That would put anyone on edge a little.

Her mum Michelle, best friend Alex, Shannon and the chef Phil are all characters in different ways whose company I also enjoy when I plant myself on 'my' seat. It's funny because in the past, having frequented many coffee shops; I was not one to seek out engagement with the staff. Most of the time I'm happy in my own company, with the little voice in my head keeping me amused and me thinking I'm hilarious!

WELCOME TO JADE'S WORLD

Why Jade? Quite often its looks, humour and maybe even intelligence that can easily explain the attraction but sometimes it's a feeling that is much deeper and more difficult to understand. There is no doubt that Jade radiates something special. This is amplified by the fact that Jade lives in 'Jade's world' which is somewhat removed from the norm – hey everyone! Jade's world is unique, with her seeing the world through unfiltered lenses that often raise an eyebrow from those closest to her, but at the same time bringing about a smile. Just like Robyn, when she talks, she engages you with her eyes, displaying a true sense of confidence! This confident exterior does hide, at times, a tumultuous inner self. Jade's world can be a world of extremes, where the serene merges into high drama or on occasions, absolute total collapse... taxi! before returning to tranquility. In saying that, the calmness far outweighs the occasional moment of madness. When in work, her professionalism always shines through, greeting the customers with a warm smile and forever appearing calm when under pressure. I find it all engaging and fascinating to observe, quite often bringing a smile to my face.

OUT OF THE DARKNESS

As I've previously said, our personalities would appear to be schizophrenic in nature, with each of us being many versions wrapped up in one, or you could say, we are slightly different versions in every instant... take your pick. Variations in personality radiates light at different intensities. For me it's the intensity of the light within Jade that illuminates her presence and lights up her smile which I find very attractive. I know I'm not the only one who senses this. The light exists in us all. It is ultimately what we are composed of. But for some, it appears to us to burn brighter than in others. Not everyone will sense or feel the same intensity from the same individual as we all rotate the dimmer switch at our choosing. We have all encountered 'energy vampires' who suck the light out of us and can leave us feeling drained even though nothing physical has taken place. I said at the beginning, I have become more attuned to energy and when I first encountered Jade, I was at a very low ebb. For whatever reason she brightened my outlook. She inspired me to 'pull my tights up', to stop feeling sorry for myself, to take back responsibility and invigorate me to continue my search to be reunited with Robyn. She will never fully appreciate what she has truly done for me.

I guess that at my stage in life, all 50 years of it and knowing what I know, I've decided to take the bull by the horns and make things happen again as opposed to sitting back and going through the motions. Some people, like Jade, just happen to draw the short straw and become the focal point to help you refocus your intention. For me, times a passing as they say, but time doesn't really bother me. I still feel twenty five... well, most days and I've a lot of living to do but when it's my time, I'm ready. The fear of your own death diminishes when you see the bigger picture and with the knowledge that if I haven't managed to rediscover Robyn in this world, I know she will be waiting for me in hers. What might appear worlds apart is in reality, all superimposed.

Fundamentally, consciousness is the power of choice. In the one eternal moment, it just keeps choosing an infinity of expressions from an infinity of perspectives all for the 'soul' purpose of experiencing itself. It does this through you, as you. Outwardly, life's about experiencing new things and creating new relationships. Inwardly, it's about finding joy and choosing the beliefs that serve your desires. It's 'your' choice!

"Everyone carries a piece of the puzzle. Nobody comes into your life by mere coincidence. Trust your instincts. Do the unexpected. Find the others."

Timothy Leary

INTO THE LIGHT

At the moment of your birth you had a glutamate dump. When you gotta go, you gotta go! No, a glutamate dump in this case is a hormonal flood that takes place within the brain of a newborn baby at the point of entering the world. Glutamate is the main excitatory neurotransmitter which sends signals within the brain and throughout the body. As a child is pushed through the mother's birth canal, an intense bright light awaits at the end of the journey. Prior to entering the light, the newborn will have grown and developed in a restricted environment of darkness. When entering the world you would imagine a whole new set of signals and receptors will need to be fired up. Then after a short journey, you enter the light. Time to party!

Hopefully you'll have a lifetime of neuro-excitatory parties before the time comes to depart. Through the vast documented evidence of near death experiences, we are commonly informed by the almost departed of a feeling of being drawn towards a bright light at the end of a long, narrow tunnel. Studies have also brought to *light* that at the moment of death, a glutamate dump takes place. Interesting or what? Would this suggest birth and death are one and the same? Even better, from your point of view, will it be experienced as a cycle of rebirths (immortality) with death only being from a biological perspective? It would appear death only raises its ugly head when you perceive another to exit from *your* experience. This not only fits with spiritual wisdom, but also the pattern of reality where birth and death are opposites therefore paradoxically the same with life being a continuum (spacetime) – connecting the two as one.

"We know today man, essentially, is a being of light."

Prof Fritz-Albert Popp

Spiritual wisdom, near death experiences and altered states of consciousness when brought on by various drugs, all concur that out of body experiences can take place. Many people who have had such, recall being in the presence of God, some higher power (usually described as the infinite) or a religious archetype. It doesn't take much digging to discover the archetype in question is typically the one related to their religious persuasion. Friends and loved ones also can be encountered, bringing about an overwhelming feeling of love.

A few years back, a national newspaper headline read something like "Evidence that Jesus awaits us in the afterlife". A young girl around 6 years old had a near death experience and after being revived, told an incredible story of meeting Jesus. Whilst sitting on his knee she was told to go back as it was not her time, or words to that effect. A beautiful story, wonderfully articulated by the child, whom I believe from her point of view, was totally true. What struck me, as I continued reading, was it transpired that her father was a minister in the Christian church. Stories like this and there are many of them, convince me your own personal narrative continues into the afterlife, at least for a while. This would appear to include all of the sub-conscious programmes you have amassed. When you think about it your sub-conscious programmes are far greater and more varied than your limited conscious belief system. The sub-conscious mind acts like a tape recorder with the record button constantly on from the moment of your conception, until I guess your brain has been starved of oxygen. Research has shown that your sub-conscious records everything, not just what you have focused on in the moment, but fills in all the blanks of the peripheral picture you engage with. This, I believe is the quantum field which en-*light*-ens your picture of reality. Many people have returned with the most amazing and vivid impression of infinity – a world without division - but words fail them when they attempt to impart this experience. All would appear to be transformed by the experience.

THE POWER OF BELIEF

After Robyn's initial diagnosis, we spent the next few days in the hospital before she was allowed home on the Saturday. Less than 24 hours later we were back, this time fearing the worst. During the night, Robyn suffered a seizure which over the next few hours slowly sent her into a coma. Karen and I were in bits. We were allowed to stay with her but no information was forth coming, which led to a complete sense of helplessness. Eventually Robyn was sent for another CAT scan which confirmed a build up of pressure on her brain. To release the pressure, a shunt would have to be inserted. A half hour later a young surgeon turned up. We had to sign forms allowing the procedure to go ahead and in the event of any mishap, no legal action would be taken on our part. We were told there were four possible outcomes, with the best being Robyn would awaken straight after surgery and the worst being that she might not pull through. I was thinking how only a few days earlier we were told she should have a minimum of six months, now we might be saying good bye to our precious daughter. Life can be so fucking cruel! Having signed the forms I noticed the surgeon joke with the nurse in attendance. I could have gotten angry due to the circumstances but I felt quite the opposite. The fact he seemed so at ease helped to strengthen my belief that Robyn would come through this terrible ordeal.

As Robyn was taken to surgery, I was overcome with the feeling that I had to get as many people to pray for her as possible. I pulled my phone from my pocket to access my contact list, to discover it was out of charge. On top of this, so was Karen's – you couldn't write the script. The feeling I had to do this was overwhelming. For a moment my heart sank, before asking the nurse if they had any Nokia phone chargers. My spirits were lifted immediately when she said they should have, as people leave them behind regularly. She pulled out four chargers from under the desk but to my dismay, none were Nokia. The nurse began to apologise before, with one last grapple, she pulled out a charger hiding at the back and lo and behold, it was a Nokia. The relief I felt was immense. The feelings inside were some of the most powerful I had ever experienced. I knew in my heart I just had to do this. I spent the next few minutes sending a text message to everyone on my contact list which also included a few randomers – we all have them, but I didn't care. I informed them about Robyn's emergency operation and asked could they pray for Robyn's recovery. The moment I had finished I was enveloped with a sweeping calmness. You would imagine the next four hours would have been utter hell, but it wasn't. It passed as if it was 40 minutes. I felt totally at peace. When the doctor came into the room, I didn't brace myself, I just knew. He looked at us and smiled saying Robyn was awake and everything went very well and we could go down and see her. In that moment I felt an oasis of bliss. I just knew a higher power was at work and I sub-consciously also knew it was working through me.

I now realise this higher power is inside all of us. This is your spiritual self, a wholeness which connects not only us, but everything else. It is the power and co-creator behind the creation of the story you are always telling yourself. This power has no religion, it worships no God, and it just is and always will be. If the mind can't box it, it can't define it! It is this power which affords you the power to choose. Your reality tunnel is a co-creation between you and this infinite power supply, with infinite being the key, as it can never be switched off. *You* can turn off the switch to your projected reality tunnel and the light fades, but you are always connected to the internal power supply forever and forever more. The awareness you hold within you is this power supply and when telling your story, from your perspective, you become the self-aware aspect of this pure awareness. You are the infinite reflecting an individuation of itself for the 'soul' purpose of experience. When you awaken to this, you will realise your true potential, but with the caveat that it's always potential due to the trickster in the room. A saboteur who always lurks in the background, continually in every moment, attempting to pull the veil over the truth. This, my friend, is your greatest enemy and yet at the same time your greatest ally. Who is this trickster?... it is what you perceive as your own mind. We are all *aware* of this at some level due to it *being* a tangled hierarchy of awareness and mind. You could say this is the ultimate *being* - a fractally embedded tangled hierarchical subject – object expression. Here we go again, get the dictionary's out!

Mind... your mind (I guess you know what I'm going to say next - they are one and the same anyway) is very complex, yet functions from a simple set of quantum laws. It is the same pattern fractally embedded within itself and the one I have continually alluded to throughout this book. Fundamentally the mind defines through opposites, but as complexity increases and the opposite of something becomes vaguer, it defines via association. It is for this reason that we judge and label things differently due to our own unique experiences and what they mean to us – this allows for infinite diversity. From this, we develop our own belief system (opinions) which conditions us into believing what *we think* to be true. Ultimately there is no universal truth; there is only your truth (from your perspective). Fundamentally it's live and let live.

When creating the story of your life, you form beliefs and it's these opinions that erect the mental prison walls that constrain your own story, but at the same time it is your beliefs that are divine in nature and are the platform from which you tell your story. In effect you are deciding what *you* believe to be true and what *you* do not. It is this two-way street that creates both joy and sorrow. People get sucked into the belief that if something worked for them, or if they have had a particular experience then it must be absolute fact. As I've said before there are no facts, they are just opinions from your own unique perspective. The trick is to develop self serving beliefs that create the most joy and let go of any sub-conscious beliefs that keep you rooted and depressed. The author Robert Anton Wilson claimed to have taken it to the next level by attempting to dissolve any beliefs he once held and tell his story via his opinions. This can be done of course, but requires a very unique attitude.

"I don't believe anything I write or say. I regard belief as a form of brain damage, the death of intelligence, the fracture of creativity, the atrophy of imagination. I have opinions but no Belief System (B.S.)"

Robert Anton Wilson

With mind being the skeleton in the closet, you become unaware that it is you who is choosing everything. The other hurdle you come up against is the bench mark of what is joyous. What I mean by that is, if you are always creating things that you like, it doesn't take long before the things you once enjoyed become boring. This, I believe is the default setting to encourage you from your spiritual perspective; to broaden your experiences. As I've said, spirit yearns to know itself in all its magnificence through you in every way imaginable, but you are the opposite. Your ego is formed by the beliefs you hold the strongest and the habits you exhibit. You see, the ego is the illusion you believe your biological self to be but you are not your ego. This is the trick mind plays on itself to evolve.

Evolution is a fractal pattern spiralling back and forth, taking quantum leaps recursively to higher and lower dimensions. This dance is fundamentally a kaleidoscope of light. Consciousness via mind somehow objectifies this kaleidoscope into the reality that we perceive and at the same time creates a story deciding what it all means in an infinity of ways. This is why, from our perspective, light can be measured both as a wave (wholeness) and a discreet photon (individuation). Light is a reflection of you. You are a being of light as well as light 'being'. You are whole and complete from a spiritual perspective whilst simultaneously an individuated activity within wholeness connected to all other activities. In other words there are always two opposing points of view that can be taken, with an infinity of views in between.

Mainstream science can never embrace this, as it always looks only from the human perspective. Christianity hits the same brick wall as it personifies God as some all powerful being separate from you. This is best exemplified by the biblical text that we are made in the image and likeness of God - with God quite often appearing as an unshaven bloke in the sky that looks just like the next hobo! Come on! What if... image is short for imagination (image-in-action) and likeness is 'light' (every 'thing' is light)? In this case we are the personified oneness of that which cannot be named – the infinite! We are in essence the imagination of ourselves.

My dream, many would say is impossible. The dream to bring Robyn back to life; the dream to change the past. If I haven't convinced you by now that it's you who is the power behind the story you are telling yourself the likelihood is I'm not going to, but that's ok. The Universe abhors a vacuum; it always fills it with something. There is no such thing as empty space, hence it requires every perceivable perspective to fill the void and that includes those who see it differently. If everyone suddenly believed the same thing, evolution would stagnate and die. If you are a sceptic, your narrative will always fit your scepticism – life by design is a self-fulfilling prophesy! What I'm proposing is not a belief system, but the *pattern* that allows every belief system to flourish. It's totally up to you what you believe; this is your divine right.

MY DECIMAL DELUSION

Ten years ago I believed time was controlled by some sort of universal mechanical clock. That the present moment preceded the future and that the past was set in stone and there was nothing any of us could do about it. Ten years ago I believed what the western mainstream media, for the most part, was spouting; basically we're the good guys and all of our enemies are the bad. Ten years ago I believed that recorded history like the past was set in stone and that it was undeniable, never questioning who might have written it, for what gain and from which perspective. Ten years ago I believed western medicine was the dog's bollocks and that the ultimate goal of the pharmaceutical giants was not about profit, but human health. Ten years ago I believed a solid real world existed whether I or anybody else was present or not. Ten years on I realise all of the above is a delusion of mind. Ten years ago mainstream science, as it is today, was telling us we have no special place in the universe, that we are insignificant and that a Goldilocks universe has arisen by chance. Ten years ago deep inside, even then, I knew that was bullshit. Ten years ago I was not religious; ten years on I'm still not. But what I can tell you without doubt and after many years of observing the pattern of reality, is that a higher power must exist and you are not only forever umbilically connected to this power but you are also the source! Exactly ten years ago, at the time of writing, my world changed forever when we were informed of Robyn's condition.

Ten years on, where does this leave me in my quest to find Robyn? Personally, I believe very close. Knowing the world is not solid and time is not set opens up my mind to limitless possibilities. The difficultly still exists because of the sub-conscious programmes that have amalgamated throughout my lifetime continually running in the background. To change a belief you must eliminate the old to create space for the new to flourish. If you don't, a conflict occurs and the programmes tend to cancel each other out, quite often leading to confusion.

YE MUST HAVE FAITH!

To take serious control of your life, you must become a mastermind. Not one that's full of useless neutral information, but one that can see the bigger picture; one that can be totally focused on it's objective whilst not being swayed by other's limiting beliefs and one that removes all barriers to dream and achieve what others believe to be impossible. How long will this take? No time at all, yet paradoxically whatever you decide.

When the doctors brought Karen and myself into the room telling us there was nothing they could do, in a state of shock I kept repeating, "There must be hope, please tell me there is hope, even a little hope". They just sat in silence shaking their heads until one of them told me to pull myself together, act like a man or words to that affect. For a split second I considered removing his head from his shoulders but thankfully my rational side quickly kicked in and when he finally, wisely said there is always hope, I managed to regain my composure.

This experience has convinced me, even when everything might appear totally hopeless; somewhere in the darkest corner of your being there always resides a little hope. All you need is just a little hope, from the smallest acorn a great Oak grows. Never ever give up hope, I know I never will.

Faith, like hope only requires the smallest of seeds to play out when wedded to expectation. You see, if you don't expect the outcome you hope for then you really have no faith in it. In a lot of cases we think we have faith in the desired outcome but if questioned what percentage is the expectation, rarely will we say 100%.

> *"Faith is the substance of things hoped for, the evidence of things not yet seen"*
>
> *Spiritual wisdom*

The mainstream scientific view hates faith... why? There are two main reasons with the first being; it cannot be measured, which is one of sciences core principles. The second is that it empowers the individual and deconstructs (shits upon) a collective materialistic world view. Along with faith you can throw in love, beauty, compassion, empathy, intelligence... the list goes on. The fact that none of these awareness traits can be measured implies (to all but the most brainwashed) that there must be something greater and more fundamental than the God of science.

In todays age many misconstrue what faith actually is. Especially those who believe themselves to be atheists and tarnish the word faith with the belief that it is solely to do with religion or a belief in God. Not so. Every one of us exhibits faith in every moment. Atheists who don't believe in a deity must have faith one doesn't exist. Science has faith in its core principles of observation and measurement. With science telling us sub-atomic particles are composed of 99.99999% empty space and with all objects being composed of such particles, we all must exhibit faith when we plant our tushes on a chair in the hope it will support us.

"Anybody who has been seriously engaged in scientific work of any kind realises that over the entrance to the gates of the temple of science are written the words: "Ye must have faith."

Max Planck

You see, you have faith in yourself... always! Both positive and negative. You have faith that your beliefs are correct but if you come to realise what you believed to be true, might not be the case, you then exhibit faith to alter your belief. Always remember, that these beliefs are only your opinions playing out from your point of view. Life tends to play out as a self fulfilling prophecy with most people hanging on to their world view for grim death, no matter how absurd it becomes. There is no right and wrong – there is only your opinion.

REALITY CREATION

Reality creation, like everything in life, is a threefold process. It is all about how you have been conditioned, relating to your environment, and what you think and feel about each experience. Remember you always and in all ways have the power of choice, not only (consciously and sub-consciously) choosing the experience, but also what that experience means to you. As I've said, take control of your mind and become the master! When you start to think negative thoughts, change your mind. When you feel good on the inside, you will resonate like experiences on the outside.

Due to change being built into the equation (spirit craves to experience all of itself) it is inevitably a challenge to maintain feeling good. In a relatively short period of time the good feeling fades and the innate desire to get it back requires a refocusing of your thoughts. Chemically, feeling good in a physical sense comes in the form of serotonin or dopamine hits, but hormones are not the source. The source is metaphysical not physical. The source is the real eternal *you*; the silent witness experiencing what *you* think and feel; the observer behind the veil. It is not the superficial external reality of your creation, yet paradoxically, this is what it becomes. When you get to grips with this, you realise you have the ability to create miracles in your life but with the caveat that this also is paradoxical.

"There are only two ways to live your life. One is though nothing is a miracle. The other is as if everything is."

Albert Einstein

Due to the nature of duality, paradoxes can arise in two ways. The first I've discussed throughout the book is because of the law of opposites, with opposites being fundamentally the one essence from an opposing perspective. The second reason that paradoxes arise, is due to points of view with each point of view creating a unique reality tunnel yet always connected to every other reality tunnel. From your point of view when you create something extraordinary this might appear to you as a miracle, but to another this might be the norm – hey everyone!... Sorry it's become a habit!

You see, pretty much everyone would say it would be a miracle if Robyn was to come back to life. These things just don't happen. Yes, on the surface this appears to be the case but only to a point. That point is related to the depth of how far you're willing to go. You can never truly know another's point of view, only your own. You create your personal reality tunnel which you could say is an extension of your own personality. You bring versions of other people into your reality tunnel that you engage with, but at a deeper level the other people are just versions of you. You can conceive of a consensual reality where others appear in agreement, but remember, this is always and in all ways only from your perspective. Once again, reality always plays out from the fundamental feedback loop system – a tangled hierarchy – of the one and the many (infinity), with you in this case being the one and everyone else the many.

To reiterate - God is one and at the same time is composed of infinite divisions, which are you and me but simultaneously you are the one, with God being the infinite divisions i.e. you and everything else. Do you get it? You are God, or for people who struggle with that term, you are "all that is". There is nothing you are not. Can you begin to appreciate the power you hold within? This being the case, can you see how you really are your own worst enemy? The time has come to change that way of thinking and become your own best friend. Let go of any victim complex! It is only you who creates and it is only you who can take responsibility to change it. In the case of my daughter, it took me a long time to accept this.

As I write these words, I now know Robyn never truly died. She *appeared* to die in the story that I constructed, but Robyn lives on in other stories as well as her own. We make the mistake in thinking that to bring about change; we must control what is going on around us. No! Change occurs naturally in the world we construct. To influence change, we must tap into the guiding winds that come from within. The winds of change flow through each and every one of us, with us having the power to affect the direction of flow. In saying that, we are not only the *director* of our story but also the *writer* and the *producer. We are the whole story.* This *is* the wholly trinity – the cause and effect, as well as the story in between.

"Be like water"

Bruce Lee

Now is the time for me to re-write my script; to take control of my 'inner voice', my 'self talk' and divorce myself from the story I have been telling. Now is the time to dream the impossible and resurrect my daughter; to retell my story, but this time with Robyn up front and centre. No *stone* exists for any story to be *set*. In truth, reality is nothing concrete, nothing material, it is only the material you use to tell the story you delude yourself into believing, that appears concrete. This revelation opened up my mind to the realisation that I do not have to prove to anyone that Robyn is alive and well in my reality tunnel because what I believe to be true will play out consensually with everything else I have created. This applies to us all. If you fall into the trap of believing that you must convince others, you give your power away due to doubt. To know without doubt is to experience that which you know. Let's stop doubting who and what we truly are and become that which truly is.

"All that we see or seem is but a dream within a dream."

Edgar Allan Poe

ONWARDS AND INWARDS

I have come to the conclusion I like coffee shops more than the coffee itself. I do like coffee, but I would choose to frequent a coffee shop more due to its ambience and vibe over the quality of its coffee. I very rarely get a take away coffee. For me it's all about the relaxation; nice comfortable surroundings with something going on around you. In a twisted way I can focus better when reading or writing with a little atmosphere as opposed to complete silence. Silence is for meditation, it has its place. Finding the balance of relationships in life is the key to a healthy, happy life whether that relationship is with a person or even a cup of coffee.

When I find a coffee shop I like, I tend to sit by the window assuming there is one. I am aware that I'm drawn towards natural light, especially since my spiritual awakening. Natural light has a very positive effect not only on the human body, but the psyche too. (At a deeper level they are one and the same anyway). As the months have gone by it feels as if I have been drawn away from the window by this 'inner' guiding light and into the inner sanctum of Crème; the hub where Jade and the gang congregate when business is slow.

Jade and the Crème crew

Like I said I have my own seat, at least 'I' think I do. I have grown to feel quite at home now. The banter is great and it breaks up the week providing me with a little oasis every now and again. As time has passed, Jade and I have become friends. It goes to show that age really is no barrier. Forming new relationships in different surroundings has helped to quash the jadedness I had been feeling. It only takes a little spark to ignite a raging fire, quite often from the most unexpected source. Jade, I thank you from the bottom of my heart. You have been the catalyst in lifting my spirits, brightening my outlook and strengthening my resolve to never, ever give up hope and continue on my quest to be reunited with my daughter Robyn.

THE POTENTIAL TRUTH

Your past and your future are not written in stone. Every possible future exists and due to it all being connected in a feedback loop, it means every possible past must also exist – right at this moment! The secret lies in awakening to the truth. The truth is everything exists *potentially*; therefore nothing exists except that which *you* decide exists in that moment. You are not in a universe; you are the whole universe, every last 'bit'. You are the most powerful being that exists, as you are 'all that is'.

At source, life is a game of hide and seek. Outwardly, you search and search for the answer you desire without realising *you* are the answer. It's like Jackanory - it is all make believe. You are making it up as you go along. If you constantly worry about losing your job, the likelihood increases that you eventually will. You have the power to tell the greatest story you can imagine with you also being the power sabotaging that story. This is life's great quandary, from your biological point of view. If we all not only realised the truth but lived our grandest vision, we would be dead to the world. In fact we would never have lived, for without death and destruction we could never be reborn. Life must recycle (feedback) for without this recycling process, life could never have existed in the first place. We see it everywhere, ashes to ashes, dust to dust is a perception you hold of recycling at the atomic level. Information cannot be created or destroyed, just recycled; the same of course goes for energy.

Isn't it ironic that when scientists calculated the total amount of energy in the universe they discovered it was a sum total of zero, which you could say is *nothing.* The universe is nothing and *you* are nothing – just the potential to be, right now! You decide what to be or not to be. You do this at the speed of light, creating retrospectively (retro-causally) a story. The story always changes and due to your magnificence, through your imagination and perception of your imagined experience, your brain acts as a step down transformer to correlate a story. It slows the process into snap shots or stills (spatial frames of reference) one after the other, which we perceive as a timeline. You see, *we* develop theories to try to explain reality but in reality they just exist as theories. Nothing tangible, just guidance. The theories paradoxically serve the purpose of making 'things' appear more concrete; nothing wrong with that.

DREAMING THE IMPOSSIBLE

We all play a role in the story we tell ourselves. At times we play the hero, at others the victim, but always the observer. From my current vantage point, seeing the bigger picture, I now realise the role I thought I was playing turns out to be quite the opposite – here we go again, my old pal - the law of opposites. I am not playing the father figure role I thought I was. The realisation has dawned on me that my role in this process is of the lost child seeking guidance to find love; the love of my daughter. I realise now that I never actually lost Robyn, all along it was me who got lost. When we do get lost, we wander around in the darkness with little or no direction until a catalyst, a spark, quite often from the most unexpected source appears to reveal a guiding light. The light has been guiding me all along, luring me into its sanctum, burning brighter and brighter. The light that burns brightest guides the way, but to see it you must be prepared to open up your heart. This light, you could say is your Guardian Angel *enlightening* the path to the way, the truth and the life of your dreams.

I feel my 'apocalypse' is nearing completion. The secret knowledge has been revealed to me. I realise now why, but that, I cannot put into words. For if I did, they would fall on deaf ears as this is my personal journey. With every story being open to interpretation, it is only you who can decide the true meaning of yours. You have your story and everyone else has theirs. So why not tell it like the God that you truly are and create the platform to spread your wings that will allow you "to reach the unreachable star, to dream the impossible dream!"

Lightning Source UK Ltd.
Milton Keynes UK
UKOW01f2353280218
318657UK00001B/70/P